ook is

future of children.

Komal Shah

RAISE YOUR HAND!

RAISE YOUR HAND!

A CALL FOR CONSCIOUSNESS IN EDUCATION

KOMAL SHAH

NEW DEGREE PRESS

COPYRIGHT © 2021 KOMAL SHAH

RAISE YOUR HAND!
A Call for Consciousness in Education

ISBN   978-1-63730-617-8   *Hardcover*

There can be no keener revelation of a society's soul than the way in which it treats its children.

CONTENTS

To my students:

You changed my life in more ways than I can say.

Thank you for inspiring me.

This book is for you.

INTRODUCTION

——

My phone buzzed quietly in my cup holder, barely audible over my radio. I turned the volume down to glance at my caller ID.

Diana?

We hadn't taught together in over a year. My mind circulated with confusion.

I picked up the phone.

"Hey Komal, where are you right now?"

"I'm driving home. What's going on?"

"Okay, I think you should pull over for this."

I could feel my heart pulsating faster, as if I already knew what was about to happen.

"Komal, I'm so sorry, but today we found Anthony's[1] body behind the school. He was shot. We don't have more information, but he died."

I could hear the hesitation in her voice; a softness that only comes with unfortunate news. Both of my hands clasped the steering wheel, trying to reach for anything that would provide pause. As I hunched over, clenching my stomach, tears began to fill my eyes.

Anthony was dead.

He was gone.

Agony overtook my "end of day" exhaustion. Pain enveloped my body as I built up the strength to drive home. I entered my apartment, gazing around the room at what felt like unfamiliar surroundings. I curled up onto my bed, staring blankly at the white wall. *Was he really dead? Was this even real?*

A sharp, stabbing pain shot through my heart. I sat there, frozen.

It was like time had stopped.

This intense feeling of grief consumed me for hours. It was in these moments of darkness that I began to reminisce about Anthony: a young, suave boy who always wore a big smile on his face. He would greet me daily with a "Hey, Ms. Shah" whenever he entered the classroom.

---

1   Name has been changed to respect privacy of both student and family.

He had graciously filled one of my seventh-grade math seats just two years prior. Anthony confidently walked down the halls, always surrounded by a group of friends who enjoyed his light-hearted company.

I remembered spending time on the phone with his mother that year, sharing stories about her son's antics and celebrating his successes. She was his biggest advocate, something I so deeply admired. The last time we spoke, she asked me to write a letter for him to our local law enforcement agency after an unfortunate run-in with the police. As a young, African American boy, the system was not always in his favor. I did so without hesitation.

Anthony was a good kid.

He deserved a second chance.

A few days after I wrote to law enforcement on his behalf, Anthony knocked on my classroom door, as I was packing up to leave for the day. "Ms. Shah?" he asked.

"What's up, Anthony?"

"I just wanted to give you this."

Anthony grabbed a purple card out of his backpack and handed it over with a heartfelt smile.

I opened it to find large, green letters spelling out, "Thank You." That one moment solidified our relationship. As I recalled this memory, reality quickly set in.

That was the last time I saw Anthony alive.

Within a few days of this terrifying news, I visited the site of his death. There was an eeriness in the air, as if his spirit was watching over the gathering. There were small candles, each shining brightly to create a shape of a heart, spelling out his name. T-shirts, hats, and other memorabilia were left out as offerings. I looked around and saw many of my students, past and present, standing tall and still. Though their faces were stoic, their eyes shone with pain and guilt.

A few days later, I attended his funeral. Grieving community members, dressed in white, filled rows of chairs. A casket lay in the front, carrying Anthony's lifeless body. As we walked toward the family to pay our condolences, children grasped their friends' shoulders, hunched over with pain as tears covered their innocent faces.

It felt like something you only saw in the movies.

The first days back in the classroom were painful. My body was going through the motions, but my insides were slowly crumbling. I knew I needed to act "normal."

Be professional.

Each morning, I tried to leave my emotions at the door and focus on teaching the lessons for my students' futures, but the classroom felt cold. My students were searching for the energetic Ms. Shah, but she was lost. In some ways, that part of her was gone.

It was time to embrace my vulnerability.

One afternoon, I hesitantly put up a picture of Anthony on a PowerPoint slide alongside his purple "Thank You" card. I slowly began to express the grief I was experiencing. As I tried to hold back my tears, I looked around the room. It was as if sunlight rays had illuminated the once dim space.

My students stared at me deeply, but not with confusion. Instead, their bodies had softened while their eyes filled with tears. A hidden tenderness had emerged. It was like the light switch had turned on, and they saw me not as their teacher, but as a human being.

As class ended, many kids embraced me with big hugs and words of comfort.

"Ms. Shah, I also lost someone recently."

"Ms. Shah, I'm so sorry to hear this."

"Ms. Shah, we're here for you."

For the first time, the veil had been lifted. After class ended, my students sat in a circle as if we were sitting around a campfire—kindred spirits gathering as a community to share their long-lost memories. One by one, each student began to share their own stories about grief and loss. My students, whom I deeply loved, were showing a part of them I for so long had ignored.

They had been putting on resilient faces to learn math.

It felt like their humanity had been stripped away from them in the name of learning.

This act of vulnerability sparked a profound realization. There was a dissonance between what I was teaching in the classroom and what my students actually needed. Every day, I focused on getting through my lesson plan: warm up, inquiry activity, main lesson, and exit ticket; yet there was no space for teaching other aspects that made up a child.

A new space where we could have an open conversation about other parts of our lives and how to navigate them. It was at that moment that I decided to commit myself to curiosity and self-discovery. I would sit down and begin to question every part of the educational system in hopes I could find the answers to create a better learning environment for my students.

My curiosity led me to discover that our public school systems were far more broken than I could have ever imagined. I saw the roots of outdated educational models constricting schools' potential for growth. I saw how the ideals of this system still echoed today.

Get good grades.

Go to college.

Get a job.

Seeing these ideals still emphasized shook me to my core.

How was this applicable to today's kids?

I realized the core focus on academic achievement as a way of schooling children has cycled through generations. The reality is that academic success is just one kind, and, as studies have shown time and time again, this often comes at the expense of children's emotional health and well-being.

I've discovered the key problem in today's schools is that the focus on academic success has limited our students. Instead of nurturing the love of learning, we have created a competitive space only focused on IQ; a space that associates a child's self-worth with a test score or a grade.

Ultimately, a number.

I believe we can create something different and build an educational system that focuses on children's inner self as opposed to their external, marketable success.

This would be a world in which we would celebrate each child's unique gifts, nurturing the core aspects of who they are as learners. To realize that compassion and love reside within us all, and that each child has an inherent value in our society.

This includes discovering whom they are, finding their purpose, and ensuring they become conscious contributors. A world in which we set up future children for real success: living a life of authenticity and true alignment to self.

So how do I fit into this?

It's because I was the teacher who followed the rules. I had colored within the lines and taught to the test. I embodied the educator who perpetuated a certain ideal of success without questioning its origin. It was subtle, like pressuring my students to get good grades or creating pacing guides that supported the "one size fits all" model. It was as if I was more concerned about working within the system rather than working for the students.

It's not until I realized my grief for Anthony that I began to question the entirety of the educational model. I had to question whether my role as an educator was building the foundation of the whole child. If it wasn't, why?

It was uncomfortable, but necessary.

This process meant I had to go against the grain of what an effective educator looked like within the system. It also meant I had to look deeply at my conditioning from growing up to see how both the purpose of education as well as the ideals of success were communicated to me. As I reflected, I began to make some shifts in the classroom through small actions.

I started with tactics like morning check-in questions, addressing emotions, and integrating mindfulness practices. This energetic shift in the classroom happened gradually. I witnessed students internalizing the benefits of calming techniques and tools. Students began to slowly learn to recalibrate themselves, leading to heightened focus for the rest of the lesson. The consistency around vulnerability and emotions led to a powerful message that enabled my students to connect with themselves. It was a conscious education in the making.

Something I wish Anthony had been given access to before his tragedy.

After five years of teaching, it felt like I had planted a seed that would hopefully grow in the years to come. Through this experience, I deepened my journey of self-reflection. I was given a new perspective of the power of connection with oneself. I now have a unique lens on the problems within the current education system through my own learning as an educator. I feel enabled to foresee a new possibility for the future.

I strongly believe that the education system has the power to shift the trajectory of our children's futures to have conscious children become conscious adults.

This is how Raise Your Hand! A Call for Consciousness in Education *was born.*

Through this book, I intend to explore the intersection of consciousness and education, shining a spotlight on not only the problems within the current education system, but a renewed focus on the whole child. Providing a vision for a new generation of children who are compassionate, empathetic, and empowered in their lives.

All children deserve a more conscious education.

I invite you on this journey with me to explore how we can shift education, not only for our existing students, but for future generations to come. Whether you're a teacher, administrator, parent, or a former student, it's important to acknowledge that we all have a complicated relationship with our education.

This book is intended for anyone who wants to change this system for the better.

To all of you who are reading, thank you so much for being here and joining me on this journey. I believe that with the current state of our world, there is an urgency in exploring a different way of educating our youth. I hope that by the end of this book, I leave you with more curiosity and open-mindedness about how we can cultivate consciousness in our students.

This vision is different.

I am happy you're here.

PART I

THE WHY

1

WHERE IT ALL BEGAN

———

"If we teach today's students as we taught yesterday's,
we rob them of tomorrow."

-JOHN DEWEY

A sea of students shuffle through a locker-filled hallway, laughing and carrying on as an upbeat teen anthem plays in the background. They slowly make their way into the classroom and take their seat in a row of numbered wooden desks, rummaging through their backpacks for pens, pencils, and notebooks. A bell suddenly rings, and the anthem cuts out. Silence fills the room.

The teacher, a matronly woman, wears large, black-rimmed glasses, eyebrows raised, waiting impatiently. Her ruler taps on the pale green chalkboard, gesturing to the homework assignment from the night before. As she begins her lap around the classroom and subsequent lecture, we pan to the students' once lively faces. One throws his hood over his head and pulls the drawstrings tight. Another lays their head down on the desk. The rest stare straight forward, their eyes glazed over.

No one is listening.

No one is engaged.

The bell rings and students shuffle out as the teacher shouts the homework for the evening.

Sound familiar?

There can be skepticism that this type of education system can actually exist in the twenty-first century. Having desks in rows and students sitting quietly seems like a time in the '80s. But here's the thing—It's not.

Though some schools with means have changed the built-in environment for their students through project-based learning and integration of technology, very few have innovated their models. To this day, many millennials and Gen Z populations can put themselves into a school scene of any movie just like this one, regardless of when it hit the box office. It's their reality, and not one that speaks to their own true life.

With several generations of students having encountered the same type of schooling, we have to ask:

How has our past dictated our present and future?

In order to create a vision for consciousness in education, we have to look back at historical times and understand where this all began.

It's important to note that before black-rimmed glasses and yardsticks were invented, learning was an organic process. It was mostly passed down from families, tribes, or apprenticeships. There were no limitations, and this was seemingly the most natural way of teaching.

No mandatory school. No mandatory system.

This all changed in the eighteenth century in Prussia (modern day Germany). This was where the original idea of compulsory education came about when Frederick the Great, a Prussian King, issued a decree where education was mandatory in rural communities. At the time, the intention was to teach soldiers (and future soldiers) basic literacy skills. (Zinkina, Korotayev, and Andreev, 2013)

It was as if compulsory education was born as a product of war. What was once organic teaching became used as a part of formal training. The tactics were based on fear and control, and primarily for militaristic needs. Eventually, the purpose of education became nationalistic in nature, where children were taught shared values to unify the country. In other words, it was to generate loyalty through obedience.

In the name of unity, many students at these schools lost themselves in the process. This push for a national identity was the first remnant of our children moving from individuality to conformity.

Johann Gottlieb Fichte, a German philosopher, was the brain behind this new model of schooling. It is important that, at the time, providing free schooling was a novel concept to all German citizens. The hope was to build a new middle class and it was revolutionary; however, manipulation was the key driver to this idea. Fichte states:

"Education should aim at destroying freewill so that after pupils are schooled, they will be incapable throughout the rest of their lives of thinking or acting otherwise than as their school masters would have wished," (Freedom in Thought, 2017).

Schooling was for the benefit of the government, not the individual.

By the time the Industrial Revolution arrived in the nineteenth century, education had evolved into a tool for economic gain. There was a massive surge in demand for workers in factory jobs. The surrounding countries jumped onboard to educate and train workers into specific jobs that required a single function. The focus was on productivity, as well as systemized control to ensure a streamlined process. ("The History of Education," 2012)

Many of these types of schools were one-room schoolhouses, where hundreds of students gathered in a common hall. One teacher disseminated information in the front while students took detailed notes and listened intently.

Again, sound familiar?

Many scholars refer to this one-room schoolhouse as the "factory model." They have expressed their contempt for this style of schooling, arguing that its design was only intended to create "docile subjects and factory workers."

The system was built towards the efficiency of children— products rather than learners. It was the perfect assembly line. The most optimized products made the end of the belt, and others were thrown away in the process.

The modern-day good or bad student.

When Horace Mann, "The Father of American Public Education," came in the 1840s, this exact Prussian model intrigued him. At the time, Mann was on the Board of Education in Massachusetts and had his eye on the prize to bring home a revolutionary educational model.

Though Mann was aware that the Prussian's model was based on "obedience of authority," he felt it just needed to be put in the right hands. The standardization of education in the US was officially set in motion by 1870; however, there was a lack of consistency between various cities in the country. In order to bridge this gap, The Committee of Ten was created. ("The History of Education," 2012)

Here were ten gentlemen from Harvard who asked the following question: "What should happen in twelve years of compulsory education?" The committee did extensive research and collaborated with many colleges. Subjects and pacing guides were eventually created: Geometry in tenth,

Physics in eleventh, Civics in twelfth. Thus, came our modern-day K–12 curriculum.

This is when learning became defiled, in a sense. In the name of standardization, children were ripped from their interests and desires. It's safe to say that these ten men decided what we learned and when we learned it. We still use this blueprint to date.

The history of our education system shines a light on the fact that it was never intended to support the whole child. Our children were never asked what they wanted in the process. It was instead created to fit the mold and impose values of the nation and society at large. This is how we've come to see benchmarks, testing, and ideals of future success.

It's about the system's needs, not the children's.

Sir Ken Robinson, founder of the Creative Schools movement, shared in his 2006 Ted Talk, "Do School's Kill Creativity?" that today's schools are still organized according to the original factory line:
- Batching students by age
- Separating subjects by grade level
- Switching classes with bell rings
- Emphasizing the individual rather than collaboration

Why is this a problem?

We still push a model that values efficiency over mastery. Noam Chomsky, an American linguist, spoke to this in his 2012 talk, "Education Is a System of Indoctrination of the Young." He emphasizes that children are taught to be passive, only given a gold star when they are obedient. If a child pushes back, they now become a "behavioral problem." The problem lies in a modern world where uniqueness and innovation are rewarded, yet the opposite is taught for twelve years in a child's education.

How can a child cultivate a sense of self when they've been given no tools to do so?

As Ellwood Cubberley, an educational administrator, shared, "Schools are in a sense factories in which the raw materials (children) are to be shaped and fashioned into products to meet the various demands of life," ("Why Is the School System Failing? The Future of Education," 2017).

The remnants of this factory model are also seen in the design of our physical schools. Many of the designers of our schools in the US were also designers of prisons. "These rectangular, closed off classrooms suit the old educational paradigm and serve little to stimulate and nurture knowledge," (Valencia, 2020). If you've been to a traditional K–12 school lately, this same layout exists.

Although we have made some strides in educational reform in the past few decades, this factory model remains at the root of every modern school system. As is often said amongst educators:

"The system is doing exactly what it was meant to do."

Yet, the world has progressed, and we are still holding onto an outdated view of compulsory education. Though many progressive movements have tried to push for innovation in the field, these are small remedies to a greater issue. The outdated educational paradigm still stands tall within the system.

Public schools have an underlying thread of the specific mindsets of our history. Many schools still model teachers as authorities and students as obedient learners. There is a push to conform to specific ideals of success. This is then measured through standardized tests. If our system is a product of history, we have to stop and ask ourselves:

How has this affected our students?

Jaya Das spoke to this reality.

For Das, a former monk and now co-founder of Good Luck Yogi, school meant nothing. At the age of seven, Das sat at a desk, day after day, being taught subjects with no real relevance. He knew there was more to life than what he was learning. In his words, he saw the word desk as a metaphor: *Discourage every single kid.*

Das struggled to learn content irrelevant to his interests and passions.

"I had no interest in the traditional standardized system. I always sat in the back of the class. I would wear a hoodie while I would be doing graffiti and writing rhymes in a notebook."

Das had never been given the opportunity to discover his own gifts, thus being ostracized by the system. His story is a similar reality to others, no matter the generation or region of the world.

Sadhguru, an Indian philosopher and yogi, had the same sentiment as Das when he shared his experience in school while growing up in Mysore, India. ("Watch Sadhguru's Experience of Education with CEO of EduComp, 2013)

"When I first went to school, I had no clue why I [was] going."

This remark echoed in a packed room as Sadhguru spoke about growing up in a culture where education was considered sacred. In order to appease his parents, he attended his local schools; yet there was something that caused resistance within him, even as a young boy.

"I always found in the school, teachers were talking about something that doesn't mean anything to them. So, my ears were never with them."

Even though he felt negatively towards school, there was no choice to do something else. He was forced to go to school day after day, but what he learned was irrelevant.

For both Das and Sadhguru, school was pointless. Two individuals from different eras, and yet the feeling was mutual.

School was mandatory, but not internally moving. It was a place they were required to go, but it was limiting to one's self and identity.

Where was the purpose behind the learning?

To this day, millions of kids still encounter this massive alienation from themselves by the education system; a system built centuries ago with a different purpose in mind. The words *I hate school* still echo in every classroom, principal's office, and living room.

I had an AP History teacher in high school. Though he was good at teaching the curriculum and preparing us for the end-of-year AP tests, his classroom was always fraught with tension. Students sat straight up in their chairs, their pencils frantically taking notes from his tired lectures, terrified to miss a single minute's worth of content. From the outside looking in, you'd probably think it was the ideal classroom.

He talked. We listened.

Only his students knew the truth. We listened because we didn't want to incur his infamous wrath.

This may seem like a small tactic to keep students in line, but it wasn't. Every one of us felt on edge. We all tried not to slip on the thin ice. The hairs on our backs would rise whenever we stepped into the classroom. I, for one, would come to class early, take a seat, and show that I was ready to learn. I was fearful of disappointing another adult in my life.

It was either follow the rules or be sent out. There was no middle.

I saw this similar method of schooling when I became a teacher. Many of my colleagues were proud of their class-rooms, centered on tension and disciplinary action. Count-less students would be afraid of that one teacher, sometimes saying things like, "I'm going to get kicked out anyways."

This fear was because of the power dynamic between the teacher and child. Many educators I interviewed shared with me their similar experiences about this "all-knowing" teacher. Anxiety rushed over them when entering certain classrooms, and they were scared of being shamed for not paying attention to a seemingly meaningless lecture. In either case, the fear was potent.

Fear is a living and breathing entity able to paralyze its prey, or even worse, cause it to believe the lie that accompanies it. It is a threat that triggers our fight-or-flight response, one in which the sympathetic nervous system prepares the body to fight or flee in an event perceived as stressful or frightening. ("Fight or Flight Response," 2021) Many times, this nervous system can become over-activated due to anxiety or other conditions.

In our educational system, this fight-or-flight response is triggered in a different way:

Fight: Refuse to accommodate to the educational model of being the student behind the desk.

Flight: Conform to the educational model but sacrifice one's authenticity to be accepted.

There is no other choice. We unconsciously ask children to decide between two options:
1. Be accepted by others for being "good." *or*
2. Stay rooted in your own authenticity but sacrifice a community that could support you.

This is also known as normative conformity, where a person publicly accepts the views of a group but privately rejects them. (McLeod, 2018) When the former is chosen, the indoctrination shuts off a child's capacity to question the system in the first place.

As Das passionately states, "I have never been to jail, but I have been in the public education system."

So, what are the long-term effects of a factory and fearful educational model?

Children become adults who internalize the need for permission to create their own path. This internalization of fear leads many adults to struggle to listen to the beat of their own drum. This holds true when a whopping eighty-six percent of adults are dissatisfied with their jobs in the workplace. (Clifton, 2017)

So why are adults having a hard time leaving if they're unhappy? It's the messages we receive when we're young.

"Everyone else is doing it, so you should too."

"It's the only way you can live comfortably."

"It's better to be safe than to try to risk your lifestyle for something else."

The history of our education system still affects children today. We are told what to do, rather than to pursue what fills our hearts and souls.

It's time for a new way in the twenty-first century.

A system based not on fear, but on compassion and engagement.

A system based not on external validation, but on inner self.

A system based not on obedience, but on authenticity and a joy of learning.

If we have learned anything from our past, it's that history should never be repeated.

2

THE RACE TO THE TOP

"Success is not in what you have, but who you are."

-BO BENNETT

The competition starts early. Moms try to get their kids on the list of certain preschools while pregnant, they have them in three to four activities a week while toddlers, and it just keeps going. The next thing you know, the kid is in high school with SATs, college applications, and ten extracurricular activities. The unfortunate truth? You've been told that if you stop, you'll be left behind the finish line. It instills "I'm never enough."

This race to the top has become the modern-age idea for success. People have been working tirelessly to reach a certain destination, only to have found themselves in jobs that feel meaningless. The fear of not being enough creates a scarcity mindset that feels so real. Next thing you know, anxiety kicks in and becomes the driving vehicle for this endless pursuit. So, what happens when we continuously compete, spinning the hamster wheel year after year?

Stress. Exhaustion. Burnout.

Despite knowing the effects, why do people work so hard to attain this illusion?

It's because this competition is normalized from a young age.

This is what Amna Mazin, an entrepreneur and mother of two, shared with me when she found herself struggling with her own journey of hustling.

Amna was high up on the totem pole while pursuing an engineering degree at the University of Southern California (USC), a top-tier college. You could find her listening attentively to professors during lectures and studying relentlessly at night for many exams. Postgraduation, she pursued a career in IT consulting for three more years. After receiving rave performance reviews, she was quickly promoted up the corporate ladder. In every way, she was successful. She got everything she wanted. This was true happiness.

Nevertheless, something was missing.

As she described it, it felt like she was just putting one foot in front of the other. She had become addicted to perfectionism and productivity, like a moth to a flame. She felt like a robot. And the system had, ultimately, let her down.

Specifically, it was the education system. Mazin was that child who stared at trees, played in the dirt, and loved to build sandcastles. When she entered school, this all changed. The message she received daily was how to prepare herself for college and build material wealth. There was no room to nurture other aspects of her. Over time, her childlike qualities got lost in the shuffle. Instead, her identity became attached to grades on her report card, the college she attended, and her distinguished major.

In time, Amna was forced to stop and reflect on the trajectory of her life. She was twenty-four and had a shiny new car, lived in a luxurious condo, and was financially independent. Everything was perfect—but it didn't feel like it.

"I can't explain it in words, but I felt that there was this sadness, this emptiness."

Realizing her feelings about her success were misaligned, Amna made a decision that most struggle to make. One day, she sat down and wrote a note to herself, saying that if she "felt like [that] in one week [she was] going to do something about it."

A week later, she called her manager and asked for a three-month leave of absence.

This decision was painful. Her friends and family disagreed with her decision. *How could she step away from a good job and money?* Amna stuck with her decision. She began to rip apart every belief she had been taught around success. Though she didn't know where to start, she became curious. Recalling a book from her high school days, *Tuesdays with Morrie,* she knew she could regain control over her next steps.

After many late-night journaling sessions paired with emotional breakdowns, Amna decided to take a leap of faith and become an entrepreneur. Though the pathway was filled with uncertainty, it made Amna feel alive once again. It started with a dance studio, then a not-for-profit, and finally a tech application called *Hatch Brighter* for children and parents.

Amna's own educational experience had a lasting impact on her life, but the lessons taught in school had to be unlearned. She had to develop consciousness to have a better life for her child. Now, her mission is to keep her children happy and healthy and to have them make their own choices, rather than stick with the outdated idea of success.

Why is Amna's story so important?

It's because she's not the only one. Many adults suffer from this exact thing. They've achieved everything asked of them, but still, something is missing. It's as if you buy Willy Wonka's chocolate bar, only to be left without the golden ticket.

Despite the burnout and stress, we continue to spin our wheels. *It's what you're supposed to do.* Unfortunately, our schools add to this ideal, teaching students from the start that success means reaching for more, as long as it's within a confined box. Learning and curiosity become stifled.

I think back to when I heard so many questions in my own classroom.

When I stood in front of my students at the start of a new lesson or unit, I saw their curiosity arise.

"Why are we learning this?"

"When will I ever use this?"

Their questions were always valid. Our school had a graduation rate of only sixty percent—that meant a little under half of my students would never receive their diploma. My students knew this and felt like most book learning was a waste of their time unless it had some real-world applicability.

I felt like a lone soldier, out on the field with a small shield to protect myself. Here were some of my "go-to" responses:

"You will need to know this for the state assessment."

"You will need to know this for next year."

"This will build your critical thinking for the future."

These superficial answers felt like I was putting a bandage on a deeper wound; one that would be ripped off and exposed. At the time, it was the best I could come up with. Many of my students saw through these answers and called me out. They knew there was no merit to my argument. They had access to limitless learning opportunities through their computers and their phones.

What could our antiquated school system possibly provide them that the Internet could not?

Their education felt irrelevant, but it was messaged as important. As I recall these several moments and hear Amna's story, there is a problem that manifests.

We've been taught that success is attached to outside of ourselves.

The narrative is the same: work hard every day, put in those hours, and stay focused on your goals. One day, you will wake up in that beautiful home and everything will fall into the place. *Right?* Except you may look back to see how far you have come only to find yourself still lost. You are still searching for more.

It goes back to that scarcity mindset, where you believe in order to be worthy in this fast-paced world, you must continue to strive and compete. Next thing you know, your meaning in life comes from trying to keep going, instead of seeing what's right in front of you. Sometimes, we get so lost in the shuffle we lose a part of ourselves in the process. So much so that we may find ourselves feeling guilty for relaxing or taking a day off.

The school mantra, "Get good grades, do well on your tests, go to college, and get a job," supports this idea of success. Basically, check all the boxes above and you will have ultimate happiness.

Yet, when a Gallup poll states that seventy-one percent of millennials are not engaged or are actively disengaged from their jobs, maybe this rat race to the top no longer holds true. (Adkins, 2016) When everyone is trying to become the best rat in the race, is it worth it?

Probably not—especially when our children are suffering because of it. We're raising children to seek constant external validation. The numbers' outcome becomes more important than the process.

I saw this every day in my classroom. Bright smiles would always cover my students' faces after a quick "good job" or a pat on the back after finishing a task. They had an insatiable craving for a stamp of approval. The conditioning ran so deep that my students wanted to, in some ways, be validated by the school system.

Sometimes the validation was tangible; an A on a math test or a gold star certificate for reaching a reading goal. Sometimes, it was intangible, like asking, "Ms. Shah, is this okay?" or "Ms. Shah, did I do good today?" It's as if everyone had normalized that a student should associate their value with the end result, rather than the learning process itself.

When the learning is not valued, there are consequences.

The external motivation becomes a dopamine hit. It feels good at first, but then you are looking for another hit. It's similar to getting a "like" or "comment" on social media. It makes us feel excited for a swift moment before we go back to a neutral state of scarcity and lack. We are never satisfied. It's a constant craving, and it leaves many in a place of constant seeking for more rewards.

Richard Curwin, an expert in the fields of school discipline and classroom management, said there are many reasons why this type of motivation doesn't work on children.

He described three that pertain to our current educational model:

- Children become addicted to outcome-based rewards and are unable to do work without them. It's like when children are rewarded with cookies for finishing a task. There is no value in the process itself.
- Children start valuing becoming the "finishers." They just want to get it done and be the first to the finish line. There is no value in the time and energy it takes to complete it. It's all about being number one.
- Children feel increased pressure to reach specific outcomes. When they do, they keep wanting more, never satisfied. Many straight-A students may feel that way as they constantly try to strive towards that Ivy League college. (Curwin, 2012)

The focus on outcomes continues to put children at the bottom of the power structure, making them feel they must ask adults for validation. In short, their voices don't matter.

I remember hiking up a steep trail with my brother in the scorching heat. Different-sized rocks hit the soles of my feet while I feverishly panted. Sweat dripped down my tank top as the sun beat down on the back of my neck. Whenever I looked up, all I thought was: *How far? When will we get there?*

It was in that moment that I relaxed my tensed-up body and gazed down. I slowly put one foot in front of the other. Once we reached the top, my brother looked at me once more.

"See, we've reached the top, but now you're just looking for the next peak."

This is what we do to our students. We constantly push them up a trail, asking them to climb higher and higher. Even if they're tired, they have to keep going. They must consistently please others—but once they reach the top, another peak will emerge.

The results-oriented nature of our schools leads to an insatiable need to be "doing" consistently. It's this desire to keep going, forgetting it's not a sprint, but a marathon. When the finish line doesn't exist, the value of a child is depleted. These same children then become adults, trying to discover how to quench their thirst.

The other consequence of this model is the strong fear of failure. There is this idea that if we fail, the world will collapse on us; however, it is proven that failure is paired with success. As Thomas Edison once said, "I haven't failed. I've just found ten thousand ways that won't work," (Ruth, 2016). One doesn't come without the other. This fear starts young in our schools.

Lauren Pinto, an instructional leader and teacher in Los Angeles, spoke with me about how she saw testing as a thorn in the paw. To her, it's too cold.

"We're asking [students] to think critically, grow their mind, shift their perspective, and then it comes down to a number, and that number is associated with below, near, meets, or advanced. So now, your self-worth is not about all the work you put in, but the outcome that you are."

When we boil down a child's success to a test score, it becomes psychologically harmful. This is supported by Dr. Kenneth Ginsberg, an adolescent specialist. "If success is defined very narrowly, such as a fat envelope from a specific college, then many kids end up going through [school] and feeling like a failure," (Schoeffel, Kuriloff, and van Steenwyk, 2011).

It's like when a child receives a score of fourteen out of twenty on a test, and they're only able to see the six they got wrong. In their eyes, they are a disappointment. Then there is the added layer of receiving a grade, making a child feel like they now have to walk through the hallways not with a badge of honor, but a badge of failure.

This success model in our schools continues to program our students to be fearful of failure and taking risks. They learn how to walk through the maze, hoping to avoid any road-blocks along the way. This avoidance comes from a place of fear rather than hope. Our children deserve to see their worth beyond external benchmarks.

Let's redefine success where consciousness is integrated.

I call this inner success. This is a type of success not outside of you, but instead within. Instead of trying to seek validation from others by aspiring for rewards, we are instead content with our own processes and journey. This doesn't mean there is a lack of ambition in life. What I mean is that we can perceive success differently.

Success can be defined as any of the following:
- Living life based on someone's true, authentic self
- Learning to embrace life fully (including all the ups and downs)
- Discovering the joy of the learning process

In other words, success encompasses the entirety of a student's being.

With inner success, a child feels expansive in their learning abilities.

With inner success, a child understands the value of the process.

With inner success, a child is not in competition with others.

It's about intrinsic motivation. It's about value systems. It's about passion and purpose.

More than ever before, the urgency to create a better schooling system has come to life. Since the start of the COVID crisis, our education system has been forced to innovate and mend its many flaws. This shift has been compounded with the intense feelings of despair and hopelessness that have surfaced amongst communities and humanity as a whole.

The mental health crisis has gone awry amongst both children and adults. Without the call to develop a different type of educational model, society will continue to fail to see the light at the end of the tunnel.

The time is now.

3

A PUBLIC HEALTH CRISIS

——

"Act now. There is never any time but now, and there never
will be any time but now."
-WALLACE D. WATTLES

A group of campers settle down by a riverbank when one camper catches a glimpse of a lone baby in the water going downstream. He immediately dives into the river and rescues the infant. But as he returns to shore with the baby in hand, a second camper spots another baby in the river. Then another. And another. Due to the sheer volume of babies, the campers rush to gather others for support.

Before long, the river is filled with helpless babies and a group of frantic rescuers trying to come to their aid. Though the rescuers work tirelessly to fetch the babies, they aren't able to save them all. Even worse, many rescuers drown in their efforts. After a while, the group creates a full-scale rescue operation, building hospitals, schools, social support services, and more. After all, they must do something to help all those babies they fished out of the river.

After some time, one of the rescuers leaves the group and begins to walk upstream. One of his co-patriots, frustrated, runs after him and asks where he is going. He replies,

"You keep fetching babies...I'm going to go see who is throwing these babies into the river in the first place."

This story, called The Parable of the River, was popularized in the 1930s by the social reformer and community organizer Saul Alinsky. (Schutz, 2011) Despite the many interpretations, the story focuses on the human condition during a crisis. It's like every Red Cross effort during a natural disaster; whenever a problem arises, we are all prone to act.

It is our fight-or-flight response I spoke of earlier, which causes us to jump in and help. Yet, what if this rescue operation is not always the best? We become so preoccupied putting out fires that we forget to step back and find the arsonist.

This rescue operation is seen more than ever in our education system. Our schools are fighting one crisis after another, from the widening achievement gap due to social inequities to teacher turnover. One of the steadily rising issues has been the mental health crisis, affecting one in six children in the US. (NAMI, 2020)

With US middle school suicide rates having surpassed the rate of deaths by car crashes (Nadworny, 2016), this crisis has now become an epidemic. So, the question becomes, who is the "baby thrower?"

A stampede of students ran up the stairs, signaling the end of lunch.

I took a deep breath and stepped into the hallway.

One-by-one, students rolled in, high-fiving me with their post-lunch greasy hands.

I peered over at the clock—thirty seconds left.

As I started to close the classroom door, the last kid slipped in. It was Aaron.[2]

"Relax, Ms. Shah. I'm on time."

Aaron strolled into class, fist-bumping some of his friends on the way to his seat. As he pulled his chair out, a screech met the air. He sat down with a thud and leaned his head against the wall.

"Aaron, sit up please."

"Why Ms. Shah? I already know all of this."

Another day, another apathetic student.

However, Aaron wasn't always this apathetic about school. His mother shared her concerns about his slipping behavior. In elementary school, Aaron was an energetic learner, always the first to raise his hand, proudly waving his reading certificate whenever he reached a new goal. He was the model student in many ways.

---

2   Name has been changed to respect privacy of both student and family.

Once he reached middle school, however, every lesson was perceived as a "waste of time." The focus on test scores and grades took away Aaron's natural curiosity for life and learning. His apathy grew alongside his anguish. Along with the shift of focus in the classroom, Aaron was undergoing changes at home. When his English teacher assigned an essay, Aaron scribbled feverishly onto the pages about his father leaving his family at a young age. He had been abandoned.

Aaron was a brilliant kid.

A student wise beyond his years.

Yet he had become the outlier.

Unsupported and disengaged.

A couple of years later, I ran into Aaron with his mother and girlfriend. He sported an oversized white t-shirt, baggy black jeans, and an arm tattoo. From the look of his attire, it was evident he had joined a gang. *How did we let him down?* This child could have had a different trajectory. He could have been supported and provided learning spaces that pushed him to follow his own, unique path. Instead, he was asked to succumb to the confines of a system and its ideals.

The school system had failed him.

Every year, over 1.2 million students drop out of high school in the United States alone. That's one student every twenty-six seconds. (Miller, 2020) Even when students stay, twenty-five percent of high schoolers have shown to express no purpose at all. (Damon, 2008) These once excitable students become apathetic, detached, and not concerned about much beyond themselves.

If students are spending, on average, one thousand hours in schools (US Department of Education, 2008), is there a correlation between the education system and its effect on a child's mental health?

Test scores and grades may just be one of those missing links. Many schools take pride in the culture of achievement, where students are focused on standardized testing and grade point averages. Even so, these external benchmarks may have larger ramifications than we can see with the naked eye.

An astonishing eighty-seven percent of students surveyed in 2019 by the American College Health Association said they had felt overwhelmed at some point during the school year by everything they had to do, and eighty-five percent reported feeling mentally exhausted. ("Mental Health Toll of Academic Pressure," 2021) To overcome this stress, children turned to substance use and faced depression and a poorer quality of life.

The reality is that this stress starts young. I witnessed this in my own students.

At the end of every unit, there was the dreaded distribution of exams. I would hand a stack of papers to a student who swiftly zoomed through desks and chairs, placing the papers facedown. Each student would cautiously peel the corner of the paper. A written score out of twenty would stick out at the top. Two phrases popped up in the room:

"YES!" with both arms raised high, or "Ugh, as always" followed by a shove of the assessment into the bottom of a backpack. It was in these moments as an educator that I cringed. I knew a child had once again associated their self-worth with a number.

And this was probably not the last time.

A study on the theory of intelligence shows that when students experience bad grades, the amount of cortisol, the so-called stressor, typically spikes. For most students, it drops back down to normal levels a day later, but for some, it stays high. (Terada, 2018) Standardized testing also shows an increase in cortisol levels for students, with sixty-one percent of psychologists in New York stating that the level of anxiety has increased since the inception of the Common Core State Standards. (Simpson, 2016)

"[Today's students are] the most tested generation in history," (Abeles, Rubenstein, and Weinman, 2016).

There is also the side effect of low self-esteem. Children quickly find themselves in two boxes: "I'm smart" or "I'm dumb." Over the course of their schooling, this four-walled box dictates how a child perceives themselves and their value. It has a compounding effect when the low-test scores and bad grades continue, eventually making the child feel they will never be good enough.

When I talked with Dana Overcash, a middle school counselor for over twenty years, she described how the mental health crisis has been getting worse amongst the students she works with. Every day, she sits in her large office across from young children who are weighed down by the pressure of school. The worst part is that they are afraid to tell their parents.

"I hear so many times where parents say, 'I never did this when I was in school. I always did my homework.'"

Of course, the parents mean well. *This is what it takes to become successful.* More often than not, however, it places even more fear in children. I experienced this in my own home. Growing up with immigrant parents, education was of the utmost importance. I would crumple my report card at the bottom of my backpack before my parents could scold me. *How would I get into a good college now?*

Parental pressure to excel can have a negative impact on a child and can increase a kid's risk of stress. This leads children to believe that if you fail, you won't be accepted by your loved ones. (Lee, 2016) Many times, this anxiety and stress are normalized as a part of both the schooling and home environments. In current times, 7.1 percent of children are diagnosed with anxiety every year. (Centers for Disease Control and Prevention, 2021)

To Dana, parents hold onto expectations of their child from mindsets of generations past. Many times, it's not their fault; it's just what they were taught. It may be that they grew up in a strict household when it came to education, and thus, they feel this is what is best for their child; or they see other parents boasting about their child's accomplishments and feel they must do the same. The reality is that this may only be intensifying the mental health issues we see in our children.

Take, for example, a young four-year-old child. They are usually eager and have wide eyes. You can find them playing hide and seek, pointing up at the clouds, or swinging on monkey bars. However, by the time they go into the K–12 education, there is a gradual decline in the love of learning in the classroom, similar to Amna's story.

The pressure to achieve increases rapidly, and many students begin to lose their curiosity and conform to the ideals set by the educational model: rote memorization, irrelevant lessons, and strict rules. Students are like rows of military soldiers, lined up in silence, waiting for the sergeant's cues to make their next move.

The apathy only screams louder, just like Aaron's.

In a 2008 survey of public high school teachers, twenty-nine percent of them ranked student apathy as a serious problem in the United States. (Benders, 2011) With the gradual increase in depression and anxiety amongst adolescents, this poses a real problem.

Over the past ten years, Dana has seen the apathy grow. Standardized testing and the heavy reliance on it for students to obtain "success" is an environment where apathy can flourish. (Morand, 2020) Compound that with parents pushing their own ideals of success onto children, and it creates an avalanche of issues.

What if a child has no longer bought into this outdated system?

Children can see through this façade while they pretend to jump through the hoops. To Dana, the public education system is not meeting our students' needs and not serving or focusing on the whole child.

"I wish that reading and math were not the only gods that we prayed to because there's so much more. [We don't allow] kids to shine at school because we take something that they're really bad at [like math or reading], and then we give them a double dose of it."

So, what's the cost of this mental health crisis in children?

According to the CDC, approximately $247 billion annually. (Krasner, 2013) Though this is a multi-faceted problem, the pressure from schools to achieve and follow the rules has led to increased levels of anxiety and stress. If a child is unable to keep up or sit quietly, they are left behind. This can then lead to medication being prescribed prematurely. There are 7.5 percent of children taking medication for emotional and behavioral difficulties (Insel, 2014), primarily for attention-deficit/hyperactivity disorder (ADHD).

Eventually, these mental health issues transcend into adulthood. According to the CDC, fifty percent of lifetime mental illnesses start by the age of fourteen. The pandemic has exacerbated this problem. The loneliness and difficulty with the transition to remote learning has led to an even larger increase in anxiety amongst school-aged children.

This urgency means something needs to change.

It's possible to address some of these mental health problems at a young age; however, even if we make these efforts, we may be shortsighted.

Yes, there is a mental health crisis among children, but what if we are missing something?

Time to dig our hands into the dirt and examine the roots.

In the words of the parable, what if the camper who goes upstream to find the "baby thrower" doesn't go up far enough? What if there had been someone farther up the stream?

The mental health crisis has turned out to be an uphill battle.

Treatments for anxiety and stress are increasing in school settings.

Yet, the crisis ensues, and the children continue to suffer.

What if this is not just a mental health crisis?

What if it is, instead, rooted in something deeper?

A spiritual health crisis.

One in which our young people are being taught to disconnect from themselves.

For example, take that small child who is wide-eyed and can find joy in just about anything that comes their way: dirt, bugs, smeared mashed potatoes, bubbles, you get the picture. Slowly, over time, the individuality that is the passion inside each and every one of us is molded into the predetermined child our system is cultivating.

The school system disconnects us from ourselves.

This is a crisis so deep that children are missing their inner worth, thus compounding the mental health challenges we see today. We are so busy treating the symptoms that we have forgotten to find the root cause. The culture of achievement has given children the belief that their education and future should be based on other people's expectations, not their own.

It's like a child is a blank easel that gets splattered with paint, but the adults are holding the brushes.

The educational system has contributed to this problem unconsciously. Young children are being educated, but not in a way that identifies strongly with whom they are. Instead, they are being put into predetermined boxes, stepping inside, and settling in. The heart of this crisis is acknowledging the root causes, symptoms, and systems.

The education system is one of the "baby throwers."

Despite our best efforts to address the source of these mysterious babies, more of them are floating down the river by the minute, drowning as we do what we can to catch them. But here's the thing—I'm tired of attending their funerals. I'm tired of saying, "we did the best we could." We didn't. We need to do better.

"It is easier to build strong children than to repair broken adults." -Frederick Douglass (Tauscher, 2020).

PART II

THE WHAT

4

INNATE SPIRIT
OF A CHILD

———

"Joy does not simply happen to us. We have to choose joy and keep choosing it every day."

-HENRI NOUWEN

A spotlight shines on the stage. My silhouette emerges in the darkness, waiting patiently for the song to start. In just seconds, I begin to glide from one side of the stage to the other. Expressive hand gestures float above my head, while my hips move to the rhythm of the music. The stage light illuminates the gold bangles on my wrist, while a traditional Indian skirt and blouse adorns my body. Bold hues of pink and orange softly dance all around me.

I look out at the audience as a big smile illuminates my face.

They know what I know.

I am alive.

Growing up, dancing on stage was the one thing that gave me pure joy. When I was not in school, I was performing. I used to sit in front of the TV, mesmerized by every Bollywood movie resembling a modern-day musical. Every "stage act" would have a dancer dressed in vibrant colors, lip-syncing to a new, energetic song. I was hooked.

My mom played a big role in my love of dance. From a young age, she enrolled me in Indian classical dance, even when it was a one-hour drive. She always prepped me for every dance performance, cheering me on from the sidelines. She hoped to keep me connected to my Indian culture; my roots. Little did she know, it would also connect me with myself.

Dance wasn't just a connection to my body, but to my soul. Every time I performed, I unleashed the dormant spirit that was waiting to fly; however, this embodiment was short-lived. When the stage lights turned off, I was back at school.

I would enter any classroom door and, hesitantly, walk towards my assigned seat. My backpack would open to the required supplies for the day: pencil, notebook, and the day's homework. The routine was the same. Take notes silently while staring at a washed-out whiteboard. The teacher would stand in the front teaching their lesson, as if this was their throne. None of it was exhilarating. None of it was relevant. And then there were all the rules.

Raise your hand.

Line up straight.

Don't speak unless spoken to.

This was someone else's stage, not mine.

Yet, I knew how to play the game well. My parents, who had emigrated from India, believed one thing: education was the number one gateway to success. There were no ifs, ands, or buts. In many ways, I wanted to be the perfect daughter, so I did everything asked of me. I spent hours completing my homework assignments, staying up late to check my papers for any imperfections. I was a model student.

While I loved seeing them happy, something was missing.

The student who once had a love of learning was long lost.

Every lesson I learned lacked passion or imagination.

It was like I was living a double life.

When I danced, I had creativity and freedom. When I was at school, limitations and rules confined me. It was tiring, but my parents reminded me that the latter was the only way to succeed. School felt more like a responsibility than a place of real learning. It was like a checklist that needed to be ticked. By the time I reached high school, the pressure became more serious.

One day, my parents sat me down at the dinner table and told me I needed to get serious about my studies. It was time to pick a good career. I was confused; I was only fourteen. I didn't know what I wanted to pursue, but I knew one thing.

"I want to do something that makes me feel like I'm dancing on stage."

My parents stared at me in silence, their eyes sunken in with despair. This was a foreign concept.

In their minds, a job was a responsibility to provide stability and security. It was a means to an end. It was not a vehicle for discovering your passion in life.

In order to oblige their desires, I took the safe route in college. I majored in Biology, on track for pre-med. By my junior year, I was still confused about my path. I decided to take a break from the uncertainty and go on a family trip to India to visit grand temples with a group of travelers.

At one of the holy sites, I looked outside the car window and came face-to-face with a number of distraught children. Their faces were smeared with dirt marks, while ragged clothes hung loose on their malnourished bodies. Their small hands reached out, begging for money. I rolled down the window to ask one of the young girls:

"Why aren't you in school?"

"We don't have a school here."

I looked at her in confusion.

How could a community not have a school?

If she didn't have access to a quality education, who else didn't?

If students do have access, was it still considered a quality education?

These questions ran through my head on the flight back home. My previous reality had been altered. It was like not seeing a school made me see it in a different way. How could I move forward with biology when something inside of me was screaming to go in another direction? If it wasn't health-care, what was it?

It was then I saw an application for Teach For America, a two-year program that prepared you to become a teacher in an underserved community. I applied two hours before the final deadline. A couple months later, I got in. The direction of my life changed, and I never looked back.

In 2013, I stepped into a classroom for the very first time. As a young teacher, I was eager to support the innocent faces that would be looking up to me for guidance. While teaching in a hot summer classroom, I became preoccupied with learning the components of a good lesson plan while building relationships with my kids. I was also a showman, creating new and exciting performances to keep the students engaged.

As time passed, my spirit shifted. It was as if a new flow of energy was running through my body. I would bounce towards my classroom, excited to teach a new lesson to my brilliant students. A smile never failed to appear, even on the hardest of days. There were still piles of grading, difficult behavioral problems, and pressure to fulfill standards. At the same time, all of that was overshadowed by my alignment with the work.

I was alive once again.

My spark from dancing had become a spark for teaching. I had discovered a part of me that had been dormant for too long. The same dancer who would glide on stage now slid through rows of desks, presenting to her students. It was a state of pure joy. Aligned with the mind-body-spirit connection, I had rediscovered that spirit aspect once again.

The spirit of the performer.

The spirit of the dancer.

The spirit of the authentic self.

It was as if the unconscious became alive in my consciousness.

I finally peeked behind the curtain of external validation.

The deeper sense of connection I discovered was one I wanted every child to feel.

It made me wonder: *how can we nurture this innate spirit that lies within every child?*

Is it possible within the education system?

Lisa Miller, the author of *The Spiritual Child*, has done in-depth research to define spirituality as "an inner sense of relationship to a higher power that is loving and guiding," (Miller and Barker, 2016). She talks about this 'core human endowment' and being able to nurture it in kids during adolescence, to prevent issues including substance abuse, anxiety, and depression [in the future]," (Collins, 2016).

In this day and age, spirituality has many definitions and meanings. The one I speak of steps away from the higher power and is instead about connecting with oneself. In other words, your inner world. Think of it like a filing system. There is a cabinet filled with green hanging folders storing your papers dating back years. Each of those documents contains various memories and emotions that have happened to you throughout your life. This filing system becomes your reference point. When anything happens to you, your brain is busy sifting through the folders to see whether it should react or respond. It's up to us to figure out how this system works.

As famous author Eckhart Tolle said, "Being spiritual has nothing to do with what you believe and everything to do with your state of consciousness," (Tolle, n.d.).

Our inner world is a part of us, but we haven't had the space to nurture it. This spirit within—emotions, self-love, and authenticity—guides whether we experience life to the fullest. It's like waking up every day excited to go to work. When we can understand the complexities of our inner self, we have a chance to live our lives with more happiness and contentment. Many times, this process includes self-discovery and reflection. It's an evolving process, and one that many children are naturally attuned to.

This inner world is all about addressing the entirety of the mind-body-spirit connection of a child.

The mind-body connection, as described by Johns Hopkins University, is the belief that our emotional health and mind manifest into physical symptoms. It's like when we get butterflies in our stomach before going up on stage for a speech. There are social and biological factors that affect our body ("The Mind-Body Connection," 2021).

Dr. James S. Gordon, founder of the Center for Mind-Body Medicine, further explains: "...[we] share a common chemical language and are constantly communicating with one another," (Gordon, 2021). This suggests that the different systems residing within us are interconnected.

Our feelings create thoughts that create behaviors. A basic example is when you feel angry about your day and end up being irritated by your spouse and yell at them. Unconsciously, we harm others around us.

With a spiritual health crisis identified before, we must look critically at our educational model. Is the model supporting connection with self or disconnection with self? In many ways, the latter holds true.

When I spoke with Kelci Hart Brock, a parent of two and co-founder of EPIC Life Learning Community, she spoke about how we have to honor each individual in their uniqueness:

"Each individual has their own authority, their own path and purpose, and they come in with consciousness that is innately aware of this truth. When we honor and nurture the unique, aligned choices and path of each individual, we naturally begin to move away from structures based mostly on competition and toward a new sense of what it means to be connected to ourselves, to a community, and to life itself."

To Brock, education is unique for each child, and it's up to us to support each individual meaningfully in developing their gifts and navigating their challenges along their own life path within a community that provides care and belonging.

Most school systems shy away from cultivating this innate spirit of a child in the classroom. I remember constantly being told about the limitations of instructional minutes and discouraged from integrating this aspect of learning for a child. My job was simply to get my students to score well on state assessments.

Prepare them for college. For their future. For their success.

We prepare them for the future, but we miss who they are today.

This expectation to push them along the same path as the previous generation is infuriating to me. Are we going to continue to ignore the cries from our students to give space for deeper connection with self, or only push a model that says math and reading are the sole forms of learning?

There is a way to focus on the mind-body-spirit connection of the whole child.

Renowned psychologist and child development theorist Jean Piaget states, "Our real problem is—what is the goal of education? Are we forming children that are only capable of learning what is already known? Or should we try developing creative and innovative minds," (O'Leary, 2019).

Play-based learning is just one of many examples that provides space for students to explore and be imaginative. This is a type of learning where the teacher encourages children through inquiry and interactions aimed to stretch their thinking. Not only that, but children are naturally motivated to play. (O'Leary, 2019) This type of learning in educational spaces enables children to open up their innate curiosity.

Not only that, but children don't feel like they are in competition with others. This type of learning is active and in real-time. It's like teaching a child how to be kind versus having them volunteer at a soup kitchen for the weekend. This type of organic learning will always be impactful. When this happens, a child's brain develops and starts to make sense of the world. They learn not by what others tell them to do, but how they choose to define it. They learn to trust their inner world.

Another example is secular mindfulness exercises, which have been on the rise in educational spaces. Mindfulness exercises provide a tool for children to pause, reflect, and connect with their breath. This is a key part of the mind-body-spirit connection.

Megan Cowan, the co-founder of Mindful Schools, spoke to me about her ten-year experience bringing secular mindfulness training to both educators and students starting in 2007. In her perspective, there are some problems existing with cultivating the inner world of a child in the current schooling system.

She explained that progressive, alternative education like Montessori and Waldorf schools have a foundation that children should be cultivated holistically. The environment created is set up to let the children experience themselves and follow their own motivations. It's built into the philosophy. This is, however, fundamentally different from public institutional education.

"It's really hard to support the spiritual side and inner life of a child [in these spaces] in a secular way. The forces are too big and the messages countering it are larger."

Through the implementation of mindfulness programming in the K–12 space, Cowan saw that the message was that the inner world is not as valuable and important. It was a half-baked attempt to support the students, but the outer world would always take more merit. Even so, the work of Mindful Schools has resulted in one hundred percent of teachers seeing a change in their student's overall well-being. ("Community Impact," 2020)

However, to uplift the consciousness of children, it does begin with the inner self.

As Alison Gopnik, a developmental psychologist, would say: "The child is not an empty vessel to be filled with expert knowledge, but an agent who acts upon the world around them," (Fisher, 2021).

If we were to integrate consciousness into education, the individual learner would be the focus. We would cultivate the true essence of who they are, instead of what we're trying to make them become.

How do we go about doing this?

It starts with first identifying our beliefs about education and its purpose. If we want to cultivate the holistic student, it begins with unlearning ourselves.

5

PEELING BACK
THE LAYERS

———

"Recognize that unlearning is the highest form of learning."
-RUMI

Christopher Latham Sholes sat in front of his typewriter with frustration. As both a printer and inventor, Sholes couldn't get over how often the keys would stick together whenever he typed too quickly. After many attempts, all met with failure, Sholes caught a glimpse of something peculiar. The same couple of keys stuck together.

That's when a light bulb idea struck.

He realized he might have found the solution to one of life's major annoyances.

Sticky keys.

He went ahead and ended up rearranging the keys on his keyboard to space out the most frequently used letters so they weren't right next to each other. (Pistorius 2020)

Little did he know that his invention would work so well that we would be using it 150 years later!

This "no sticky key" keyboard is now known as the modern QWERTY keyboard; however, since the origin of the keyboard, there have been many complaints about the ergonomics. Many inventors have tried to redesign the keyboard and enhance it for modern times. New prototypes have frequently come out with different letter combinations to support typing efficiently. The DVORAK keyboard even showed a seventy-four percent speed increase, with a sixty-eight percent increase in accuracy. (Bigler 2003) Yet, each time, the market fails to adopt it. The problem? We've all learned to type a certain way. It's practically part of our DNA.

Behind the story of the invention of the keyboard lies an important truth.

As humans, we have a difficult time abandoning ways of established thinking and acting.

Also known as unlearning.

"The only thing that's harder than starting something new, is stopping something old," (Ackoff, 2015).

We all know about our habitual patterns.

Why is it so difficult to stop something old?

It all comes down to our brains and how they're wired.

When we learn something a particular way and can repeat it over and over again, that task becomes, for all intents and purposes, automated. The billions of neurons in our brain build stronger connections over time, and those tasks become instinctual. This includes our daily routines. We are on autopilot; meaning ninety-five percent of our actions are the results of everything we have already learned. (Kanwar, 2020)

Waking up in the morning.

Brushing your teeth.

Driving your car.

The more we do it, the less energy we use so we can focus on more important things. In many ways, this benefits us and allows us to become more productive and multi-task. The way we initially learned those tasks becomes ingrained in our subconscious.

However, there is a flip side to this learning. Certain ways of doing things stick to us like honey due to comfort level and routine. Even worse, certain ways of thinking stick to us even when it becomes outdated. This is harmful when it no longer works.

It's as if these repetitive situations become thoughtless acts. For instance, take a grocery store. In the back is the warehouse stocked with new goods: canned beans, gallons of milk, and cartons of eggs. Why? Because out on the shelves are goods with pending expiration dates. Those new items are always available to make sure we avoid a crisis that may arise from spoiled milk or rotten eggs.

This also pertains to us as humans. If we as individuals don't take a regular inventory of ourselves, we have layers of learning that become spoiled. These once-learned behaviors need to have a regular check-in appointment to ask ourselves if we have passed the expiration date, or if we're still good for another year.

Some of these layers of learning run deep. It begins with learning to ride a bike to eventually learning to navigate the world. We then develop how to think, feel, and act, and this conditioning takes time to uncover.

Take, for example, gender norms and how they are perceived in the world.

Justin Baldoni, an American actor and filmmaker, shared about masculinity in his 2017 TED Talk. His father, a role model of Justin's growing up, was a man who had a softness to him. This meant he didn't teach Justin to hunt, how to fight, or do other "manly" stuff. Justin resented this because the small town he grew up in bullied him for this softness.

He was seen as not "man enough." The one thing that was considered a "strength" in his family, however, was Justin hiding his feelings.

"A lot of us men are really good at making friends, and talking, just not about anything real. If it's about work or sports or politics or women, we have no problem sharing our opinions, but if it's about our insecurities or our struggles, our fear of failure, then it's almost like we become paralyzed," (Baldoni, 2017).

After thirty years, Justin woke up and realized he was living in a state of conflict. He didn't want to fit in the current broken definition of masculinity to be strong. He wanted to just be a better human who could balance both aspects of himself.

In other words, he had to unlearn to relearn.

I had to face this as well. I had to unlearn to become a bride-to-be.

When I was little, I was taught that being a bride was something to aspire to. My mom and I would spend hours planning my future wedding. We had every last detail down. I would walk down the aisle in an expensive red bridal outfit and gold jewelry while my groom would wait. Hundreds of guests would greet me on either side, with flowers and cameras in hand. Heck, even acquaintances would be there to celebrate my big day.

It would be the greatest moment of my life.

Yet, this aspiration only led to subtle internalizations. I began to believe that my only value was becoming a bride and, ultimately, a wife. Generations of women before me had walked down this exact path. And so would I.

Except, every time this came up, feelings of anxiety rose and my stomach clenched. This fantasy didn't feel expansive. Instead, it felt like I had shackles put on both my hands and feet. Even though it felt misaligned, I lacked the courage to find a new path.

Who would love a spirited and outspoken girl? Who had bigger dreams than a bride-to-be?

As I continued to live out this false narrative in both high school and college, I became more curious. Questions arose in my head like never before.

Did I even want to get married?

If I did, did it matter what age it happened?

Was my sole purpose in life to become a bride and then a wife?

Suddenly, the picture-perfect wedding my mom and I had been planning started to fall out of focus. All the traditions and assumptions I had made of my value in the world were no longer true. But who was I without them?

It was at that moment I began to slowly open Pandora's box, unearthing my previously held beliefs. I began to question my role in each of them. It was liberating while also painfully scary. I finally began the process of unlearning.

While these patterns can be difficult to change, it's important to note that change is not impossible. In fact, many scientists believe our brains are more malleable than we give them credit for. Researchers at the National Alliance on Mental Illness (NAMI) describe our brain's ability to grow and reorganize information as neuroplasticity. (Harris, 2021) This means we can rewire our neurons to change the brain.

What does unlearning have to do with our education system?

Systems are made up of people. If the system needs to change, then people need to change first. It's only when we unlearn on an individual level that we have a chance to change our century-old educational model. We have become stuck in an old way, so much so that it has become run-of-the-mill. It is unconscious.

Katie De Jong tells her story in the book *The Art of Unlearning*, where she emphasizes that we get a multitude of messages from society of what it means to be a successful or good person. This is entrenched in our system from the beginning. Many of us may be products of the system. This makes the unlearning process even more difficult because our own value is attached to it.

The 4.0 GPA we got during high school.

The college diploma hung up on our office wall.

The high-tech company that gave us an offer letter (and a company card).

There is obviously nothing wrong with these celebratory moments; it shows the value of education. And many times, there is pride in this achievement. However, this is still associated with the external idea of success. As mentioned before, a success that is based on merits, benchmarks, and external validation.

If we look at this from a lens of inner success—one with happiness and fulfillment—these achievements may tell a different story. Even so, our reputations and careers become attached to this old ideal. As an article in the *Harvard Business Review* states:

"Letting go can seem like starting over and losing our status, authority, or sense of self," (Bonchek, 2016).

To begin the process to unlearn means to look at everything you once held as the truth with a magnifying glass. When we take this microscopic view, we may find resistance. De Jong explains this process further: "We first have to forget about how we used to think, and really consciously and proactively *choose* to believe and act in a new way. And it's so easy to slip back into the 'old way,'" (De Jong, 2019).

This is why, many times, these ways of thinking are passed down from generation to generation. This is even seen with parents pushing a standard of success just because it was taught to them from traditions of the past. This is not to blame, but instead, gives insight as to why previously held beliefs get passed down without hesitation.

When I spoke with Matt Barnes, the founder of The Education Game, he spoke to the resistance he faces when he coaches parents on how to adopt a new way of learning for their kids. He faces the same pushback. "The belief is that you must conform to the K–12 environment to create a successful life. You focus intently on grades, even if you don't care about the learning. You just suck it up and you do it."

This process is also arduous for an educator. The K–12 Dive Newsletter explores this by stating "[it] is often difficult because changing long-held ideas is more personal for educators and can feel like an assault on their sense of identity," (Harper, 2019).

Educators often equate their identity to their work because their work is, inherently, their life. When the system evaluates teachers based on student performance, it becomes personal. It's as if doing something wrong is calling out that they have failed as a teacher, even though there could be many other factors impeding a child's performance.

Even if educators love their students, they may become attached to their own idea of success. Thus, with their own loss of purpose, they may have a hard time questioning things that may no longer serve students well. It's as if there is a loss of consciousness.

When I spoke with Heather Cowap, a curriculum developer and science teacher, she experienced this pushback after adopting an educational framework, called Universal Design for Learning (UDL), in her classroom. Based on neuroscience research, UDL has the following pillars (Novak, 2019):

1. Students being taught based on their strengths and weaknesses, not benchmarked against an "average" student.
2. Teachers transition into the role of the facilitator, removing barriers to learning by giving students options.
3. Providing diverse forms of engagement, means of representation, and multiple means of action and expression.

When she introduced this in her classroom, Cowap was met with many resistant teachers. This was a brand-new blended learning model requiring the teacher to unlearn how traditional curriculum was taught. To her, the hesitancy made sense for this shift. "... [They] feel like they're expected to go from zero to 100." It's not the innovative curriculum itself but abandoning an old pattern of teaching that causes the problem. It's the understanding that lectures may not be the best way to teach children.

Cowap also explained how many of her student's parents were averse to the idea of UDL, associating it with a type of learning best suited for universities. She heard that students were too young and not capable enough for this type of choice. It was then she had to go back to reiterate that teaching isn't just lecture. Cowap expressed her frustration:

"We're still dealing with this archaic old vision of education. [This old vision still exists] in our movies, in our books, and in our culture. We have to move past it."

This reluctance to adopt new methods is further explained by the sunk cost fallacy: an idea where "we continue an action because of our past decisions (time, money, resources) rather than a rational choice of what will maximize our utility at the present moment," (Pettinger, 2017). When we have already invested all this time and energy building this model of education, it can feel like there is no point in trying to make it more conscious now.

Let's say we do choose to step outside the mental model in order to choose a different one. How do we go about doing it?

It starts with the willingness to challenge our beliefs. It starts with reflection and questioning. This goes not only for educators, but for parents, educational leaders, and every adult who was once a child sitting behind a desk.

Here are some critical questions to begin the unlearning process, starting with our own educational experience (which is different for every person):
- Did I like school growing up? Why or why not?
- What does success look like to me? How was it messaged to me?
- Are there harmful messages in school?
- Do I believe in the culture of achievement perpetuated in schools?
- Was I emotionally supported while being in school? If not, why?

The steps go like this:
1. Acknowledge
2. Reflect
3. Resist
4. Overcome Resistance

Again, it's scary to look at old mindsets, but this reframe is needed for every single person. It's a choice we make to shift existing structures even if we have to confront our own beliefs transcending generations. It begins with the critical work to identify and extract harmful mental models from both our school systems and us.

If we truly want to bring more consciousness for children, we have to be willing to build a new pathway. This includes neural pathways that can rewire our brains. A pathway that questions these outdated beliefs (that have reached their expiration date) to build a better system for children.

"We cannot solve our problems with the same thinking we used when we created them" -Albert Einstein (Einstein 2019).

This is because our children's future well-being is at stake. If we continue to resist this change to protect ourselves, we cannot help the current and future students thrive in their own lives for the modern-day.

Yes, I know this seems scary.

But only then do future generations have a chance to become their authentic selves in this world.

6

HIDING BEHIND
THE MASK

———

"The privilege of a lifetime is to become who you truly are."
-CARL JUNG

My large-rimmed glasses cover my small face as I curl up on the beanbag chair in the corner. The new Nancy Drew thriller lies on my lap, a yellow hardback cover showing a detailed illustration of the coolest woman detective in town.

What crime would she solve next?

My wide eyes scan the words as I flip through the crisp new pages with excitement. Anticipation runs through my veins with every new adventure. Hours pass by. I glance over at the library clock and jump up within a second. *I have to go.* I stuff the half-read book into my backpack, grab my used library card, and run towards the sliding doors.

It is time to leave my happy place. A place that feels like home.

But this home is not accepted by everyone—especially by my mother.

Why is my daughter reading books instead of hanging out with her friends?

This was the singular question that ran through my mother's head while I was growing up. Every time I came back home from the library with a stack of books, I would run upstairs and lock myself in my room for hours. My obsession with reading was always met with her dissatisfaction. To my mother, extroversion meant social acceptance, not being a bookworm.

Though my mother loved me deeply, she had succumbed to an unspoken rule of the community. Being social was better than sitting behind closed doors. The problem wasn't that her daughter loved reading—the problem was that she was supposed to be a "normal" kid who liked to go out and have fun.

After many arguments, I became desperate. I decided to put my interests aside and join the tribe for the sake of peace. I knew if I shared my authentic self, even my family would shame me. All I wanted was to immerse myself in books, but the message was always the same.

Others would never accept what gave me joy.

This lost joy may have been felt by some of you at a young age. Feeling ashamed for loving something—painting on a canvas with a new watercolor palette or moving your fingers on the new strings of a guitar to play your favorite song—didn't matter. These weren't considered "realistic career choices," just "frivolous" interests. This same story occurs today. Children are forced to put their desires aside in order to conform to society's standards of success. That innate fire is burned out and joy is replaced with despair, hopelessness, and feelings of lack of purpose.

For me, I felt rejected for my interests. I decided to put on an act to be accepted. Eventually, I adopted what many call "the false self." In an article by professional counselor Laura K. Schenck, the adaptation of the false self is described using three characteristics:

- Putting on a façade with others but feeling drained.
- Seeking mood-altering substances to connect with that "different" self.
- Partaking in actions that may feel forced, alienated, or detached. (Schenck, 2011)

Every time I let go of something else that gave me joy, I felt like I was putting on a Halloween mask to hide; a shield to stop others from seeing my real self. I didn't realize that this mask would linger for some time.

The reality is that this costume becomes part of our regular attire. We become used to hiding because it feels easier to pretend than to defend our desires. It's like when I put away my books to please my mother; we want to stop trying to report to others. Even if this feels like the best short-term solution, what are the implications?

Exhaustion.

It's exhausting to play a role you are not right for in order to feel accepted. Schenck clarifies, "there is a natural human tendency to protect our authentic selves from the scrutiny of the outside world," (Schenck, 2011). It's like showing up to a high school dance in a dress and you find out it's a pajama party. We all fear being rejected or ridiculed by others. This is why we try to assimilate to our surroundings; yet, this benign gesture can cause toxicity in your development, eventually giving you a warped sense of self.

Dr. Shefali Tsabary, a best-selling author and conscious parenting expert, shares that parents are usually the first people to impose their ideals on their children. Many times, parents have their own emotional baggage from their life and ask their children to bear it. They don't even realize it; it's unconscious. Children then carry the weight and bear the burden to carry out the adult's ideal life. They then lose their authentic self in the process. (Forleo, 2018)

Why do we learn to adopt this false self?

British psychoanalyst and child psychologist, Donald Winnicott, explains that it actually begins in infancy. Since the 1960s, Winnicott has advocated that infants must be given space to embrace their emotions and live with a minimal amount of demand from adults. In his perception, if space for authenticity is not given, infants grow up to become adults influenced by the demands of their external reality. ("The True and the False Self," 2018)

The infant learns to trust itself or learns to trust its environment.

Most children learn the latter. They begin to trust their environment, meaning they raise their hands and look around for the adults to give them permission. It goes back to the externalized success model I mentioned earlier. We learn to keep striving, losing who we are in the process. Our schools add insult to this injury.

In our current model, who we really are is barely nurtured. Most schools push cultural values of high achievement and adherence to rules. In order to fit the mold, children put their dreams and desires aside and eventually adopt the false self.

Chelsea Robberson, a former school leader and educator, relayed to me her struggles to find authenticity within her school. As someone ambitious in her studies, Robberson's class schedule was filled with pre-AP and AP classes. This made her feel more connected to those in other grades, but not necessarily those in her grade level.

"I had no interest in what was going on with my peers. I was always missing that basis of a relationship."

For Robberson, her desire to build relationships only led her more into isolation. She never felt truly accepted to become her authentic self within the confines of the classroom. She decided to leave tenth grade, much to her mother's objections, to pave her own path. Now, Robberson hopes to never have her own children experience this false self as she moves them into self-directed education.

Robberson isn't the only one. Whether it is getting out of your seat without permission or asking incessant questions to the teacher, most students are unconsciously told to dim their lights. If they shine too brightly, others won't accept it. Children then shrink themselves even smaller to assimilate. The authentic self is continuously turned away for conformity.

Let's say a child does decide to stay true to him or herself—other classmates in the space may pick on them. Remember those days when you heard the words "nerd" screamed in the hallway to the kid who was reading a book, or "teacher's pet" if she raised her hand first in class? It's *Mean Girls* 2.0. The desire to fit in with others has become worse with social media. The Netflix documentary *Social Dilemma* shares, "Social media starts to dig deeper and deeper down into the brain stem and take over kids' sense of self-worth and identity," (Levitt, 2020).

Students are grasping for the mask sooner rather than later.

The symptoms of this toxic schooling become evident in adulthood. As we get older, our brains become hardwired and have a difficult time unlearning, as explained in the previous chapter. When we resist change, we have a greater attachment to a certain sense of identity, even if that identity is the false self. Think of all the comedians, like Robin

Williams, who make the whole world laugh, but are deeply depressed when alone. There is a disconnection.

In Brené Brown's book, *The Gifts of Imperfection*, Brown shares that authenticity is a daily practice. It's about "...letting go of who we think we're supposed to be and embracing who we are," (Brown, 2014). This means cultivating the courage to be emotionally honest, set boundaries, and become vulnerable. Yes, even when this vulnerability brings up shame because it allows us to tap into that "resilient human spirit."

The human spirit will always have social pressure and outside expectations. We live in a society, after all. However, if we shift our education system from pushing inauthenticity to one that cultivates consciousness, then children may not have to become adults who ask themselves, *who am I really?*

How do we identify authenticity?

One way to know we are raising authentic children is "when children act like their true selves... [This then lets children] experience increased happiness, improved self-esteem, and better relationships," (Harris, 2020). This is evident when children:
- Form relationships grounded in real connection.
- Stand up for themselves and others, despite peer pressure.
- Take full advantage of their own talents and gifts.
- Act with self-confidence, creativity, and self-expression.

These various elements of authentic children can lead to more consciousness in our educational model.

1. When it comes to relationships, these are real connections. The reality in our current system is that there is a teacher-student power dynamic that limits authentic connections. If a child goes to their teacher excited about an unconventional topic, they must feel safe enough to do so. This is possible only when adults and the young people in the space become co-creators, finding space for self-expression. Once adults tap into their own authenticity, children will learn it is possible for them to do the same. It's about modeling.

2. In order for students to stand up for themselves, they must feel empowered. As I've mentioned, schools become breeding grounds for conformity and groupthink. It's similar to the workplace, where you stay late until the boss leaves because everyone else does. To stand up for oneself requires the courage to stay authentic and have space to be vulnerable. When this vulnerability happens, empathy manifests and students feel confident to stay aligned to their own values.

3. Every student has a talent and a gift, but schools must allow for them to be cultivated. The culture must give children time to explore their interests and passions. Yes, even beyond early childhood education. This would mean having a more fluid and flexible curriculum, as well as mentorship and real-world application to create unique career pathways. Since eighty-five percent of jobs in 2030 haven't been invented yet (Tencer, 2017), this space for youth to explore is vital.

4. If we want students to become self-confident, creative, and self-expressive, it's a collaborative effort. It's also the

willingness to have students go against groupthink or think outside of the box. Can we genuinely provide safe spaces for students to share their voice and stand up for themselves, even if it's against the adults?

It's difficult because it takes putting our egos aside. We have to realize that what we believe is right for children may not resonate with them and their idea of success. The reality is this:

The child's authentic self must always take precedence over anyone else's expectations.

When I spoke with Raheen Fatima, a young student from Pakistan who reached out for an interview, I was shocked. Here was a thirteen-year-old who had taken full advantage of her talents and gifts. One glance at her Facebook profile and her personal brand stood out to me.

Stand-up comedian.

Interviewer.

Theatre actress.

Entrepreneur.

Though the schooling system didn't support her gifts, her parents did. They wanted her to go after her passions and interests and helped discover her voice. It was magical to see her voice become a beacon of light. Now, Raheen has had the privilege to interview the Dalai Lama and leads workshops with prominent figures all over the world. All she needed was the room to tap into her gifts and not hide under a mask to fulfill other people's expectations.

She had learned to trust herself once again.

It made me realize that children do have the full capacity to be themselves, but they have to be given the chance. When this happens, it is linked to greater happiness. Psychologist Rom Brafman looked into the research of clinicians in England who did a study in the *Journal of Counseling Psychology*. Authentic qualities were questioned, including self-awareness, communication style, and openness to others' feedback. After the measures, they found "the more a person acted authentically, the more likely he or she were to be happy and experience subjective and psychological well-being," (Brafman, 2008).

What does it mean to REALLY be you?

Is it creating a life where you feel excited about your partner?

Is it creating a life where you travel the world?

Is it feeling liberated or expansive?

This message can be frustrating since we've been conditioned to seek validation outside of ourselves. We are encouraged to live a life like an exclusive feature in a magazine; airbrushed and perfect. Though we often strive to feel connected to our authentic self, we end up living a life far from it.

If we want students to live a happy and fulfilled life, adults must as well; unlearn and relearn. When we do this, we can prioritize this genuine self in our children. Then students may have the capacity to live a thriving life.

It's only then that we can proudly say, "be yourself" and mean it.

One step towards living our truest selves is by embracing our emotions.

Without feeling the hurt, authenticity is impossible to uncover.

7

OUR EMOTIONAL AWARENESS

———

"In a very real sense we have two minds, one that thinks and one that feels."

-DANIEL GOLEMAN

A family sits around their wooden dining table, ready for a peaceful meal. Tonight, it's spaghetti and meatballs. As the family eats and goes around to share how their day went, something shifts. The husband talks about his terrible day at work and ends with a snide comment about the food. His wife immediately erupts in fury. She spent all day working and is desperate for some appreciation for her efforts in the kitchen.

Chaos ensues.

Next thing you know, the husband shakes his head with confusion at her reaction as he furiously puts his hands up in despair. His wife's eyes bulge as she points her accusing finger across the table. The argument goes back and forth. The tense energy in the room floats to the other family members.

On either end of the table are the couple's four- and six-year-old kids. The daughter immediately cowers under the table, while her brother bubbles up with anxiety. Both children are forced to watch their parents' rage and fury. They can't speak; only listen.

If asked, these parents would agree they love their children and do their best to make them happy. They aren't lying, they are just so used to confrontation as communication, and they think it's normal.

Little does the couple know the kids feel helpless. Trapped.

I know the feeling—I was one of those kids.

I was the girl who would hide behind closed doors, but it wasn't always by choice. Outside of my sanctuary was chaos. Family conflict ripped apart every panel in the house. Shouting matches between my parents and older brother penetrated the walls, while angry screams and cries lasted for hours. I was in the corner, a silent observer.

When the arguments would escalate, I ran to my room, grabbed my blanket, and tossed it over my head. *I want to hide here forever.* On my bed lay a worn diary. Tears streamed down my eyes as I opened the lock and bled ink onto the many blank pages.

This was my safe place.

A place where I could openly express my feelings without judgment.

A place where it felt like, finally, there was someone listening.

This listening didn't last forever. I felt the urge to share my feelings with my family, but I never did. If I shared what I felt, it would just add fuel to the fire; a fire only adding to my parents' own struggles with emotions. I knew they were trying their best, but it was better to keep quiet.

Time after time, I kept silent, never expressing my repressed rage, sadness, and confusion.

This was the accepted narrative in my house; and yet, there was hope.

School—my refuge.

But even that space didn't listen.

Immediately homework, study guides, and irrelevant lessons shut me down. It was evident by the instructional time that my cognitive and intellectual abilities were more important than my feelings. Even if I wanted to share my emotions, there was no safe space for it, so I did what others did so well—stared at the whiteboard and pushed aside my inner world.

Day after day, the feelings got worse, but I was told it was all going to be okay. All I had to do was do well in school and my worries would fly away. Just study hard and get a good grade; that is the key to happiness. My parents and teachers had done it and so could I. It made me believe that the turmoil I felt every day was just temporary.

Emotions are a key part of our conscious living. As biologist Charles Darwin once said, every emotion serves a purpose. It's part of our survival. "Feelings are like signs on the map of your internal guidance system that help you get to where you want to go," (Lechner, 2018).

The unfortunate truth is that we are conditioned out of these signs, eventually learning to suppress these emotions just like I did. Instead of viewing our emotions as a guiding compass, we learn to navigate them blindly. This then manifests into everyday interactions ingrained in us, such as our daily greetings:

"Hey, how are you?"

"I'm good, you?"

"I'm great. Thanks!"

Do we genuinely care about how someone is *actually* feeling?

In an article written by happiness expert Tamara Lechner, learning to hide our emotions is taught from a young age. To express a true emotion is viewed as a sign of weakness, even when this is foundational to someone's well-being. "You educate yourself out of your ability to feel a full range of feelings by continually pushing emotions down until you lose the ability to feel them at all," (Lechner, 2018).

This is what I saw in my home. Adults learned from their childhood that emotions, especially anger and sadness, should not be expressed. It's a sign you are not well, and others would not know how to handle them. If the adults in my world felt they couldn't express them, how would I be taught to do the same? Unfortunately, this same message was perpetuated in school and the cycle continued.

The educational model has the power to change this generational cycle.

The Collaborative for Academic, Social, and Emotional Learning (CASEL), a well-renowned organization, pushes for emotional integration in schools. Specifically, social-emotional learning, or SEL, is a topic gaining traction within the current educational model. According to CASEL, the focus on emotions can combat students' anxiety, behavioral problems, and substance abuse. ("SEL Impact," 2019) The goal is to support young people with the following:
1. Manage their emotions.
2. Cultivate empathy for others.
3. Establish supportive relationships.

"The promotion of social, emotional, and academic learning is not a shifting educational fad; it is the substance of education itself. It is not a distraction from the 'real work' of math and English instruction; it is how instruction can succeed," ("From a Nation at Risk to a Nation at Hope," 2018).

Emotions are the substance of education itself.

Our emotional awareness is not supplemental to the curriculum. It is the foundation to building engaged learners. We have been taught to tell children to put their emotions aside and focus on the lesson at hand. It's like asking an adult to do a twenty-minute work presentation amidst a nasty divorce. It can be done, but it won't be done effectively. It's a short-term remedy to a deep-rooted issue.

In *Permission to Feel*, author Marc Brackett shares his twenty-plus years of research on emotions at the Yale Center of Emotional Intelligence. He found that emotions matter, and you have to adopt a lens seeing the feelings of kids and adults in our schools as critical to success. To him, if we keep focusing on cognitive abilities, we miss a tremendous amount of information. (Brackett, 2019)

Despite the importance of emotions, many teachers and administrators are resistant to incorporating SEL into the classrooms. It's like the familiar saying, "Leave your emotions at the door." The curriculum in the classroom comes first just as your work at your job comes first, but if a child can't focus on the learning without addressing their emotions, isn't this counterintuitive?

This is not to say that educators are not supportive or don't want the best for their students. The reality is that even if they wanted to, there is no time, energy, and space to do so. During one of his workshops, Brackett stood in front of hesitant educators. In order to break the ice, he asked, "How do you feel inside your classroom?" The answers from the teachers were the same as the students.

"Frustrated, overwhelmed, stressed."

As the main facilitators of a student's learning, teachers' feelings matter as well; however, when the high stakes testing model puts school leaders and faculty members in combat between emotional needs and academic needs, it can feel like the teetering of a seesaw, and usually the academic side takes the win.

The metrics schools assess for learning also add to the problem. Think about every school that proudly boasts about their student body's GPAs, the state test scores, and the mastery of standards. Though this is aligned with the modern success model, there is no one measuring the teacher and student's well-being. It's like assessing productivity in a factory without looking at the worker conditions.

Nicolette Sowder, founder of Wilder Child, explains, "One reason we are obsessed with ABCs and 123s is because it's easy to see and analyze those results. Emotional intelligence is so much harder to nurture, support, and measure. And the truth is those types of slow-moving, ambiguous metrics really don't align [with] our work within the consumer-based society we often unconsciously maintain," (Sowder, n.d.).

This brings back the competitive nature of our world. We keep striving, forgetting to address our fundamental emotions.

Psychologist Susan David shares in her 2018 TED Talk, "The Gift and Power of Emotional Courage," when emotions are pushed aside or ignored, they get stronger. This is called amplification. She gives the analogy of trying to ignore a delicious chocolate cake in the refrigerator. As we know, it's quite impossible.

Candice Georgis, a mindfulness consultant and educator, speaks to this same avoidance of emotions in her own life.

"I had a really hard time expressing myself as a child. I went through a period of eight years where I didn't cry. Physically, my body couldn't actually do it, so I was very disassociated from my emotions, my emotional standings, and the way that I felt."

This time of suppression became hardwired. It began to affect Georgis in her interactions with others, but mostly herself. It was another form of disconnection as she went through the motions of life. It wasn't until Georgis discovered meditative techniques that she began to acknowledge these emotions and slowly uncover them. To this day, she works through the process of acknowledging and releasing emotions, hoping to support her clients with this as well.

"[I truly believe that] if you're not self-aware and cognizant of your own mental, emotional, and spiritual state...you're not leading clearly and in alignment. A lot of the time, it is going to be out of projection when something comes to you." It's like having a hard time seeing someone else cry because you struggle with your own sadness. This is unconscious behavior.

Marc Brackett continues to ask, how can we teach people to experience their "full range of emotions that make them human?" It takes a systematic approach to build a common language for emotions. This can easily be done in the school environment. Brackett created a framework called RULER to support school communities to integrate the value of emotions:

R - Recognizing
U - Understanding
L - Labeling
E - Expressing
R - Regulating

However, this framework is only as successful as the way schools integrate it. Here is his advice:

1. The best SEL approaches are systemic, not piecemeal. There is a mindset that academic achievement is far more important than the emotional well-being of a child. If a SEL curriculum is added to a school setting, it must pair with a cultural shift. It's like when a company announces a wellness week with yoga classes and healthy meals, but has employees work tirelessly the rest of the year. It's not an integrative approach.

2. The best SEL efforts are proactive, not reactive. Before we send a student to the counselor's office, can we find ways to recognize this beforehand? This is like the "baby thrower" parable in chapter three. Are we able to provide language for emotions from the beginning, instead of sending children to counselors when they act out in class? It again comes with a conscious cultural shift.

3. The most effective SEL curriculum is continuous. This means that skill building is provided across all grade

levels to reach all children. The best schools that incorporate this model follow the children through every developmental stage. When I spoke with Paula Talman, the founder of iSpace Wellbeing, a game-based design curriculum for mental health, she mentioned how she wanted to follow children throughout their school journey. This led her to work with over 270 schools globally, serving 100,000 children in all age groups.

4. The best SEL approaches pay attention to the outcome. The metrics set in place should be able to assess whether the emotional and mental well-being shifts for students over time. This is not a short-term integration. It is similar to our own never-ending healing journeys. It takes time.

These approaches take intentionality, and when done right, our children are rewarded. This work of emotional intelligence also supports the inner spirit of a child. Since feelings are our internal guidance, they are part of our conscious way of living. Dr. Kress, an associate professor, shares, "Both spirituality and SEL relate to how one interacts in and with the world." It's a key element of the mind-body-spirit connection. It allows self- and emotional awareness for a child, cultivating their own consciousness. (Elias, 2019)

Despite this, what if we continue to negate emotions for children?

These emotions will just boil over. As Dr. Tim Brieske states, "...emotions are intended to flow freely through our body-mind, then dissipate once we have fully experienced them and assimilated their valuable message...[If we continue to push them away] over time, we...have accumulated a large load of emotional toxicity that takes a toll on our mental and physical health," (Brieske, 2013).

With thirteen percent of people reporting feelings of chronic unhappiness according to the 2019 World Happiness Report, the urgency is there. The mental and physical health of adults is an epidemic, and our educational model can provide some relief to our young people. If we create conscious spaces allowing children to become "emotional scientists," they have a chance to become healthier adults.

As Mister Rogers from *Mister Rogers' Neighborhood* would boldly state, "I'm convinced that when we help our children find healthy ways of dealing with their feelings, ways that don't hurt them or anyone else, we're helping to make our world a safer, better place," (Lin, 2003).

Our children can become masters of their emotions, even when confronted with the most difficult circumstances.

8

HEALING OUR WOUNDS

———

"The greater a child's terror, and the earlier it is experienced, the harder it becomes to develop a strong and healthy sense of self."

-NATHANIEL BRANDEN

I find myself looking over at the clock every few seconds.

When would this day end?

As soon as that thought enters my mind, I am flooded with guilt.

How can I say that? These kids are my pride and joy.

The bell rings and a sigh escapes my mouth...for a second.

The day isn't over just yet.

Another wash of guilt.

Time for another parent meeting.

I hesitantly pick up my notebook and laptop and walk toward the classroom across the hall. The large door opens to a room full of teachers. I scan the table to catch the eyes of others. We all silently think the same thing.

Here we go again.

As I put my teaching materials down and grab a stool, I look up and scan the members present at the meeting. Next to me sits David's[3] mother, peering down toward her one-year-old daughter. She sways her back and forth, as if she never wants to let her go. Across from her sits David, our sixth-grade student. He towers over her with his usual oversized sweatshirt. Lately, his infamous hood always shields his eyes from the crowd. His little brother sits closely next to him, peering over the table curiously. A shy, but observant child. A mini-David. The door then opens for the final member.

The hair on everyone's arms rises.

David's father walks in. A large, stout man we hear about frequently, but have never met. As he strolls in with loose jeans and a worn-down t-shirt, I glance over at David. The young boy's body tenses up, as if he has just discovered a monster under his bed. As his father sits down next to his wife, I smell something familiar. Alcohol.

We then begin our meeting.

---

3   Name has been changed to respect privacy of both student and family.

David's behavior has declined. This is the sentiment amongst all the teachers. He refuses to do work, sleeps in class, and vandalizes property. The pile of complaints has gathered dust.

To soften the blow, we share some praises for the student we all deeply love; the boy once always engaged and excitable to learn a new lesson in class. That part of David feels long lost. These two distinct behaviors of David are alarming. So, we ask the all-too-familiar question...

Is something going on at home?

Silence.

His father glances at his family with threatening eyes, rage bubbling beneath the surface. Without missing a beat, he looks over at David and begins to scold him for this change in behavior. We sit with our eyes glued to the floor, too ashamed to look up. When his father finishes his lecture, he gets up from the table and leaves without another word. Once the door closes behind us, David's mother sighs. "It's been bad at home."

Her voice starts to tremble as she describes many traumatic incidents taking place at home. Tears stream down her cheeks as she chokes back her cries for her family. Her husband is a drunk and the emotional abuse has become physical recently. The worst part? Her sons have started modeling this same behavior. She feels helpless.

Her eyes sting as she begs for mercy. She looks at David in desperation, crying out for help to improve his behavior for the sake of the family. As the counselor slowly leads the family away for further conversation, a thought crosses my mind.

David is a young ten-year-old boy.

He sees emotional and physical abuse.

He sees the effects of alcoholism.

And yet...

What are we doing to help him?

This wasn't the first time I had sat in this type of meeting.

To be honest, this story always echoed the same.

Every parent meeting would be met with the anguish of parents, grandparents, and siblings. The difficulties at home and in the community led our students and their families to feel desperate. It seemed like every story came with its own box of tissues, tears, and heartbreak. It was in these moments I knew that the students in my classroom were more than learners. They were human beings who were suffering, and yet, there was nothing I could do.

I was stuck between a rock and a hard place. The pressures of the system still consumed me daily. Standards. Lessons. Grades. The expectation was that I wasn't a counselor, just a teacher. The curriculum and expectations overtook any type of care I could provide to my students. With a system built solely for academic achievement, the lack of integration of consciousness and tools of support created disconnection.

Here was David, a young child encountering a school intervention. Even with the best of intentions, what were the implications of this meeting? Would he go home to yet another beating by his father for not keeping his mouth shut? The support of the school would only make matters worse. David would encounter both guilt and frustration. He would feel more mistrust with the adults in his life, and he would never feel protected. The trauma would cease to stop.

To this day, the damaging narrative still exists.

Schooling and preventative support are separate.

Does our education system have more of a responsibility to support these children?

Absolutely.

This is especially true for children with trauma. However, the word "trauma" has many connotations. The reality is that it is subjective, and what may be traumatic to one person may not be traumatic to another. It also comes into play on how many traumatic experiences one endures in a lifetime. Dr. Gabor Maté, a Hungarian-Canadian physician and world-renowned trauma expert, defines the word trauma while being a guest on the podcast, *The Last Day*.

Trauma originates from the Greek word *wound*. This may be a wound experienced by great adversity, such as sexual abuse or domestic violence, and it can also stem from even smaller events. In children, trauma can be felt with something as simple as not having their feelings understood or feeling like no one spends time with them.

Dr. Maté makes a clear distinction between trauma and a traumatic experience. He shares that life brings pain, but pain is not the trauma. Instead, pain becomes traumatic when the pain isn't resolved. "Trauma is not what happens to us. Trauma is what happens inside of us," (Wittels Wachs, 2020).

If we use this definition, then most of us have experienced some level of trauma. If Dr. Maté were to ask, "Have you ever felt sad or unhappy in your childhood?" many of us would say yes. This means there is a wound unhealed due to a traumatic event. Thus, all of us have experienced this to some degree. It usually stems from childhood.

This is evident with Adverse Childhood Experiences, or ACEs (traumatic events that specifically occur in childhood). The original study took place in 1995–1997, where the CDC and Kaiser focused on three areas: abuse, neglect, and household challenges. Participants answered ten questions about their childhood and current health and behaviors to determine their score. The higher the ACEs score, the more traumatic events an individual had experienced in their life. Since that study, sixty-one percent of adults have reported the experience of at least one type of ACEs, and nearly one in six have experienced four or more types. (Centers for Disease Control and Prevention, 2020)

This ACEs crisis has also swept the nation for young people.

Of the roughly 74 million children in the US, just under 51 million are pre-K–12 public school students.

Every day, 13 million of these children go hungry.

A report of child abuse is made every ten seconds.

This is a public health crisis through and through. ("About ACEs," 2021)

What can schools do to address this?

One way is school connectedness. This is the belief held by students that adults and peers in the school care about their learning as well as individuals. To put it in other words, it's the focus on the whole child. Students who feel more connected to their school may engage in less risky behavior, including early sexual initiation, alcohol, tobacco, and other drug use. Ultimately, they do better in their learning. (Centers for Disease Control and Prevention, 2018) This is the goal we set out to achieve.

This is also vital when traumatized students are especially prone to difficulty in self-regulation, negative thinking, being on high alert, difficulty trusting adults, and inappropriate social interactions. (Lacoe, 2013; Terrasi & de Galarce, 2017) These children may unconsciously be put in the behaviorally challenged box, when they are the ones screaming for help. If many children face traumatic events, schools should create preventative spaces versus reactionary ones.

Unfortunately, many schools lack this connectedness and fail our children.

Brittany Long, who grew up in Salinas, California—a town riddled with poverty and gang violence—was one of those children. For Long, she saw how her own school was unsupportive when it came to dealing with traumatic events of children.

"I remember one year where we had six deaths of classmates due to car accidents and gang violence. Our counselors had a moment where we were asking what to do, and I could tell that our school hadn't put any emphasis on how to cope with a crisis. They hadn't really done anything to mentally prepare our students for any of the tragedies."

Long was also experiencing trouble at home. Constant fights and turbulence in her family led her to seek solace, but the downfall was bottled up emotional and mental stress. By the time Long was in high school, the emotional turmoil developed into a physical manifestation: a chronic illness. After a long stay in the hospital, she was barely skin and bones. "I didn't even have enough muscle to get up the stairs."

This is not uncommon. Dr. Bruce Perry, a psychiatrist and expert on childhood trauma, speaks to this issue in his coauthored book, *What Happened to You?* Negative experiences can derail a child's development and wires a child's brain differently. The amygdala, which is responsible for our fight-or-flight response, takes control. When this happens, it does everything in its power to keep us safe. For Brittany, her safety response was to neglect her inner world, only deepening her trauma.

Despite this, Long was determined to change the trajectory of her life. If her school or community couldn't support her, she would discover restorative exercises herself. This led her to mindfulness breathing techniques and yoga, which ultimately healed her.

"I started noticing that the more mindful I was about my body, the more mindful I was about my mind and everything in general. Since I was able to heighten my awareness, I started making my physical body better."

When Long looks back, her school could have played a critical role in her recovery. If tools were provided consistently and preventatively, she could have potentially avoided years of deteriorating physical health.

"I had manifested so much shame, depression, and anxiety. I also had really low self-esteem, but it wasn't something I could just shake off. With the coping skills, I would have had more awareness in life, and it probably would have helped me build stronger and healthier relationships, not only with other people, but also with myself."

Robert Redfield, M.D., CDC director, corroborates that trauma transcends into adulthood, with at least five of the top ten leading causes of death being associated with ACEs. With preventative care, like school support, up to approximately 1.9 million cases of heart disease and 21 million cases of depression could be potentially avoided. (Centers for Disease Control and Prevention, 2019)

Consciousness in education can support this.

School is the one safe space that can play a part in healing the wound by creating a cultural change. It's also a responsibility. The primary goal of the education system is to teach. In order to achieve this, it is sometimes necessary to remove barriers that impede a child's ability to learn. Every year, millions of dollars are authorized through various legislative acts for this purpose, including the No Child Left Behind Act of 2001. (Crosson-Tower, 2004)

To address trauma begins with building relationships beyond the classroom. Oprah speaks to this through her own experiences with childhood trauma. For Oprah, her schoolteachers provided the love and connection she needed to feel valued. This is how she coped with her situation at home. This is an example of school connectedness, which builds the foundation of a child's future. (Winfrey, 2018) The idea of integrating trauma-informed care can be a revolutionary approach and change the way we perceive our response to it.

We can go from asking, "What's wrong with you?" to "What happened to you?"

Millions of children's lives have the potential to shift if schools don't focus solely on academic learning, but the entire being. This is the responsibility of all stakeholders—parents, leaders, and teachers—within the education system to support the needs of the whole child. When this doesn't happen, behavioral problems can ensue, leading some students to end up on medication. Not only that, but children internalize that they are "bad" within the system. With preventative care, we can build a foundation for many young people who otherwise may not have the support to thrive.

As we know, if these wounds are not tended to, they become infected.

Long's story shows how lack of school intervention can affect someone's life negatively. It goes beyond a counselor's office; it's something that must be ingrained in the educational spaces themselves. It's only here that adults can address the many needs of a child. *Is this possible?*

Yes, it is and can be. After Brittany tended to her own wounds, she integrated mindfulness programming into schools in her local community. After two years, she added gratitude, kindness, and other practices to support children in not only their educational experiences but also their personal lives. She's seen so many benefits with this integration, including children sharing this with their own families when they go home. Now, Salinas' schools are even opening wellness centers to combat this problem.

If these wounds stay unhealed, the child may face a breakdown in adulthood. Internal wounds continue to bleed. This affects other aspects of someone's life. It's like an adult having difficulty building loving relationships or creating proper boundaries for themselves and others. If we keep ignoring the root problem, we will keep tending to the addictions instead of addressing the source. Those are symptoms, not the sickness. As we get older, trauma is usually passed down through generations.

"Trauma not transformed is trauma transferred." -Tabitha Mpamira-Kaguri (TEDx Talks, 2019).

According to Caroline Myss, a five-time *NYT* best-selling author, most people's consciousness journey is a result of an illness or a trauma. In other words, crisis motivated. "Pain, loss, isolation, and/or the need for personal healing drive the individual to seek out a path of personal healing, comfort, or self-empowerment. This is what happens to all those children who are feeling trauma within, especially when there is no way out," (Myss, 2013).

If schools built a foundation of our inner world, we could potentially avoid the breakdowns adults so often experience by providing intentional tools for healing and recovery; not just for students, but for teachers as well. When we cultivate conscious children aware of their inner world and trauma-informed, they can cultivate resiliency even in the most difficult times. This can lead to a new paradigm in our system.

Awakenings should not happen when we hit rock bottom.

9

THE MOST IMPORTANT RELATIONSHIP

___

"To fall in love with yourself is the first secret to happiness."
-BOB MARLEY

Kids don't learn from people they don't like.

These bold words ring in my head as Rita stands in the middle of the room fashioning a bright red blazer. The packed audience has all eyes on her, captivated by her charming and vivacious personality. She continues her speech with the poignant phrase, "We can do this. We're educators. We're born to make a difference," ("Every kid needs a champion," 2013). When the talk ends, I sit in the classroom, inspired and wanting more.

When I was doing summer training in teaching, this video would play on the screen at least once a week. It was the infamous 2013 TED Talk by none other than Rita Pierson, a teacher of over forty years. It showed every passionate educator that building relationships with our students was the number one priority. I left feeling energized, ready to inspire generations of children to come.

I set out to learn students' names, personalize my morning greeting, and look at my kids in their eyes. Every kid needs a champion...or so I thought.

It is the beginning of second period. My students are settled at their desks, staring at me with eager eyes. This is the moment teachers in my building lived for.

The calm before the storm. Minutes pass by.

The door slams open.

A young five-foot-two boy walks in; it's Jason[4]. This is the same Jason who usually spends the entire school day in the counselor's office, ditching class, and roaming the hallways.

I haven't seen him in over a week.

He storms in with a determined look. With anger fuming in his eyes, I can tell he is ready to unleash his wrath. He swiftly walks to the table in the back where the well-organized math worksheets lie. Within seconds, he grabs each stack of paper and throws them one by one. *Boom.* Holders crash while

---

4   Name has been changed to respect privacy of both student and family.

papers float into the air. The stillness in the room breaks. The other students hold their breath while the papers splay out on the floor.

"You bitch!" screams Jason as he leaves.

All the students glance at me.

How will Ms. Shah react?

There is a moment of pause. I take a few deep breaths.

I am still in shock, but the little voice inside of me tells me the show must go on.

I silently walk over to the whiteboard and begin my lesson.

Outbursts like this weren't uncommon in my school. Students had discovered that acting out could get them detention or suspension. Either way, it was time out of class and more time with their friends. A single act could lead to severe discipline, but at least it was attention. Jason was one of those students.

Jason's reputation preceded him. Every teacher assigned to him was given his disciplinary file to review before the start of the school year. It was intimidating, but deep down, at the bottom of that file, were stories that broke my heart. He was just a normal kid whose childhood was robbed from him. His family lived below the poverty line. On top of that, his mother struggled to overcome a drug addiction.

For Jason, each act of rebellion was purposeful. At home, he was an adult. He bore the responsibility to take care of his mother. At school, he put on a different role—being a child. He became someone who didn't have to face the burdens of life. With the best of intentions, this meant causing chaos wherever he stepped. Even though I knew this, it was difficult for me to not take it personally. That one negative action in the classroom felt like a personal attack, but as an educator, I had seen this time and time again.

The same students that adults in the school would label as "difficult" or "challenged" were actually the opposite. They were the children who needed the most love and nurture. Though Jason was known for his tough-guy exterior, anyone who took the time to really look at him could see the pain in his eyes. He was crying for help. He wanted to be seen.

From that moment on, I tried to develop a bond. Every time he would step into the classroom, I'd greet him with, "It's good to see you today, Jason." I showed up consistently for him. Eventually, Jason started showing up more. But more importantly, he showed up in a different way.

"It's good to see you today, Jason."

Jason enters the classroom, takes out his pencil, and begins to write down his notes.

"It's good to see you today, Jason."

Jason volunteers to pass out papers to his classmates.

Over time, the same student who internalizes that he is a "problem child" has now been seen in a new light. He finally feels like he is a part of a community.

After a few weeks of coming to class regularly, Jason once again enters my classroom. This time, the cuss words or papers on the floor are a distant memory. Today is a gallery walk. The students hold clipboards in their hands as they walk around the room to answer math questions. Jason swiftly grabs a clipboard and a worksheet. Before he begins, he waves me toward the door. Then, a flood of sincere words leaves his mouth.

"Ms. Shah, I have been meaning to tell you something. In the beginning of the year, I was bad. I mean, REALLY BAD. But now, my head is on straight again. Out of all my classes, this is the only class I work my hardest in. I just want to thank you for never leaving my side and always believing in me. You stuck with me through it all. I really appreciate it."

He then shakes my hand firmly. *Did this just happen?* I am in disbelief. The trust between us has been acknowledged, and it will take a lot to break it. Jason's words fill my heart with joy. My students often tell me they love me, but his choice to open up to me means more than I could ever put into words. This is what teachers live for...this is what *I* live for.

So why, after the initial moment of joy, do I feel so empty after?

I had been told cultivating relationships with students was the best part of teaching, especially the larger wins with students who initially are difficult to connect with. As I questioned myself, I started to realize something.

This wasn't about Jason at all.

The relationship I built with him had only depleted me more.

It made me realize that building relationships with others wasn't the problem.

It was the relationship with myself.

In a span of two years, I had taught 360 wonderful and joyful students. Without knowing it, I lost myself in the process. My once-black hair now had exposed gray stands, and dark circles hung like shadows under my eyes. My posture was tired. Every day, I struggled to keep up with lesson planning, grading, and meetings. I was overwhelmed and I had no time to stop.

I had come to terms with my existence, even if I knew it wasn't healthy. This was the state of most teachers around me, especially when, according to the Learning Policy Institute (LPI) Report, "new teachers leave at rates of somewhere between nineteen and thirty percent over their first five years of teaching," ("The Current State of Teacher Burnout in America," 2019). After a downward spiral, burnout is inevitable.

In the book, *The Resilient Practitioner,* anyone in a service-based career is seen as valuable. "Giving of oneself is the constant requirement for success...It is caring for the other, when by nature we are a species geared to needs of the self [first]," (Skovholt and Trotter-Mathison, 2011). The needs of others come before your own. For me, it wasn't sustainable.

Though I still wanted to build those relationships with my students, it was impossible because I had lost that relationship with myself. I didn't know who I was anymore.

It was time for a change.

I needed to prioritize self-care. When forty-six percent of teachers say they feel high stress daily (Turner, 2016), this was the first step towards survival. I stopped taking papers home to grade (that's right, after-hours was off). I instead used this time going to local classes ranging from yoga to meditation. Every time I stepped into class, I was forced to stop; to slow down, relax, and cut the noise in my head. It was as if every light in the room had been turned off. It was just me sitting with my inner world.

When I sat on that white, plush cushion, everything I had chosen to neglect came up. No more escaping. The first thing was the emotions. I had done a great job of burying the negative ones: anger, sadness, and frustration. As I sat on that cushion, these repressed emotions arose. I felt the chains holding me down.

I ripped open every false belief my mind had conditioned to believe, not for minutes, hours, or days, but year after year. These were beliefs that had stemmed from my childhood that I was absolutely undeserving to be loved by the people around me. Beliefs leading me to feel closed off to the world.

How could I ever love my students deeply when I couldn't even love myself?

It was this strong release, as if a sponge was being wrung out. I sat and cried. Not just for myself, but for my students. I recognized that some of the feelings I held onto were not mine, but theirs. As I began to unleash the pain and sorrows consuming me, something shifted when I stepped into the classroom. I had become lighter. And honestly, I was relieved.

As Robert Holden, a positive psychologist, shares, "The relationship with yourself sets the tone for every other relationship you have," (Deats, 2019). When I was burnt-out, I didn't realize this. It was when I took the time to stop; I began to garner a new perspective. This was when I realized my relationship with myself was the priority.

Holden continues with, "when we are self-critical, and see ourselves as deeply flawed or worthless, how can we manage to have a deep, meaningful relationship with someone else?," (Deats, 2019). This is what happened to me. Without realizing it, my lack of connection to myself filtered into my thoughts and daily actions.

I had found liberation.

I began to understand that if I didn't build a relationship with my authentic self, I would lack the capacity to build genuine relationships with others. Even with Jason, I could barely acknowledge the beauty of what we had created together.

During the rest of my time as a teacher, I kept prioritizing self-care to unleash the shadows filling my heart. I honestly didn't know it was making a difference until one day, when one of my students looked at me and said, "Ms. Shah, you're calmer now." There was a clear change in how I showed up. I was used to yelling at students who pushed my buttons (even if I didn't want to take it personally). The insides of me always bubbled up for the next explosion.

And now, the explosion was avoided by taking care of myself first. I stopped thinking it was selfish, superficial, or that I didn't have time. I did—I just needed to believe I was important enough to create that space for myself.

By my fifth year, everything had changed internally.

I was renewed.

Once I had cultivated self-love, it was time to truly give back. I knew how critical relationships were for my students. Dr. Pamela Cantor, an adolescent psychiatrist, shares that when children feel closeness, consistency, and trust, oxytocin is released. Thus, it leads to many positive effects. ("The Power of Relationships in Schools," 2019) This is the culture I wanted to create once again.

There were so many moments where I saw the shifts in both my students and myself. This included:

1. More presence in the classroom. Since I built a better relationship with myself, I was more in tune with my

students. I gauged when a student was struggling, and I checked in instead of waiting for a behavioral consequence. The students could see that, and for the first time, I was seeing them.

2. Listening without judgment. It was easy as a teacher to project my insecurities onto my students. Once I cultivated a better relationship with myself, I listened without giving advice. If a child was having a "middle school" problem, I didn't ignore it. I had learned to become a guide, providing the support needed.

3. Creating space for authentic connection. There was more intentional time and space I created in the classroom beyond math. Whether it was a check-in question or a side conversation, building relationships with students became easier and more authentic.

4. Embodiment of vulnerability. I never stopped being vulnerable with my students. I shared with them other parts of my life, constantly reminding them they could do the same. Though there was hesitation in the beginning, I shared stories to garner trust and show them that even though I was an adult, I also had my ups and downs. I was human.

The human connection is like a plant needing to be watered. This is the whole child, not just the student aspect. Skylar Primm, an educator at High Marq Environmental Charter School, shared that the way he builds relationships with his students is simple:

"I treat them like humans."

However, this is impossible if we don't cultivate that trusting relationship with ourselves. No matter who it is—a teacher, school leader, or parent—the process to create self-love will support both yourself and the student. Though this has become difficult in a system that is overwhelming and stressful, there is a light at the end of the tunnel.

How long before students can meet educators who have a strong sense of self?

It must be modeled now. It starts with the understanding of consciousness.

PART III

THE HOW

10

FROM UNCONSCIOUS TO CONSCIOUS

———

"Do the best you can until you know better. Then when you know better, do better."

-MAYA ANGELOU

Imagine you have spent your entire life in a medium-sized town. Regulars frequent their favorite coffee shops, visit the local butcher for their evening meals, and shop at the fancy stores on the weekends. Everyone knows their neighbors and traditions are always passed down.

While living in that town, your parents or caretakers have always warned you, or actually, they have forbidden you, to not venture down certain streets and areas; for your own good. You are told not to go down those streets because it's dangerous.

It's unsafe, they say.

You are taught that all you ever need for happiness and security exists only in "your part" of town. This is the safe zone. Strangely, nobody in your part of town ever seems particularly happy.

When you become an adult, you start to become curious about this other part of town. You decide you want to know more. You eagerly ask your parents about what lies in those streets. You probe and probe, only to be met with silence. They evade eye contact as they look toward the ground. "Don't ask us so many questions." It's in that moment you realize something huge—they haven't ventured past the safe zone to the other side. Yet, they still told you to never go there. Why?

It's because they had been told this same fable to be fearful of this area, and they decided to pass down that fear of uncertainty to you. They have trained you to be scared of something they themselves were trained to fear.

All unconscious.

After much frustration, you pack up a duffel bag and make the decision to listen to your gut. You are about to take off into uncharted waters. Even though people are appalled at the decision to leave, you still go. It's here you begin to embark on a journey of uncertainty in order to explore what's beyond your current reality. Once you reach outside of the safe zone, something miraculous happens.

You finally feel like you belong.

This parable is beautifully created by Craig Harper, a writer and educator, who shares his transition from living an unconscious life to a conscious one. (Harper, 2021) In Harper's journey, he makes the bold choice to leave his familiar life, like this medium-sized town, in order to explore something beyond it. In other words, he ventures out into the unknown.

As he describes it, "It's my belief that in the *process* of life, we often allow ourselves to become disconnected from our inner intelligence. From the 'know' we have beyond our experiences..." (Harper, 2021).

That "know" is our consciousness.

The Merriam-Webster dictionary defines consciousness as "the quality or state of being aware— especially of something within oneself." I've always loved this definition. It's simple. Idyllic. Concise. However, as I've learned over the past few months, consciousness may be a more complicated concept than I originally thought.

This became evident when I interviewed educators from all over the world, each defining consciousness differently:

"Consciousness is being aware of our thoughts."

"Consciousness is being aware of how we perpetuate prejudice and biases."

"Consciousness is unlearning the beliefs in our lives."

Even though each description sounded different, they still contained the same core tenants. So, how did these core tenants originate from a definition that holds true to today?

Renè Descartes, a seventeenth century philosopher, believed consciousness was a result of thought and reasoning that "because we have thoughts, we are conscious." His conclusions laid the foundation for the initial idea: as long as we could think with our minds, there was consciousness. (Jorgensen, 2020)

Louis de La Forge, a French philosopher, struggled with this definition.

What if consciousness went beyond the mind?

With his research, de La Forge began to elaborate that consciousness is not only about our thoughts but also about the inner knowledge we directly experience; knowledge of when we become aware of what we do or what takes place in ourselves. Nicolas Malebranche, another philosopher, validated this through his research, stating, "Consciousness is an *internal* phenomenon, a sensation of what is going on *in* us..." (Jorgensen, 2020).

If consciousness is truly an internal phenomenon, it must mean there is this invisible string holding us together. This string must be given attention; otherwise it becomes loose and starts to fray. This consciousness is not only through the mind but also the inner life. It's both our internal and external worlds.

Consciousness is the awareness of both worlds.

For most of us, we have awareness of our external world, especially since our environment influences us from a young age. We grow up around family, neighbors, community members, teachers, coworkers, and other people that shape who we are. We are also told to only focus on that external success. Good college, great job, and accumulation of wealth.

Our external world is put into our awareness every day.

Yet, awareness of our internal world, or inner life, may not be spoken about as much. This includes the key components we've discussed: our authenticity, our emotional awareness, and our relationship with self. It's all the things many of us are told to bury deep without a shovel in hand. The awareness of our inner world is like the intricacies of a spider web, difficult to start, but eventually you string it along. These aspects of us become silenced, but perhaps the only way to take back control of our lives.

If consciousness is the awareness of both the external and internal worlds, and one is suppressed, the question is:

Are we living an unconscious life?

When we live unconsciously, all we're doing is going through the motions. Autopilot. We wake up. Get dressed. Go to work. Come home. Eat dinner. Rinse and repeat, day in and day out, to relive this exhausting cycle all over again. This, in turn, can cause even the strongest of people to collapse under the weight of inauthenticity. Depression. Disease. Disorder.

These can all point to a deeper, unconscious issue. It's where our mind goes unchecked to repeated thoughts, patterns, and cycles.

This cycle can be exhausting until you finally decide to wake up. It's like when Neo meets Morpheus in the movie *The Matrix*, and he finally awakens to the truth. This is a conscious life, similar to what Craig Harper describes in the parable about venturing out of the safe zone of his town.

Here's the thing: we may still choose to live an unconscious life. Sometimes it's easier to be on autopilot even if it makes us sick because that's what everyone else is doing. To decide to live a conscious life means there is going to be uncertainty. As mentioned before, it's harder to stop something old, especially when no one has done it before. Sometimes, it can feel safer. There are side effects to this, however. Slowly we let go of our authentic self to fit the societal mold. It's exhausting.

This idea is supported, unfortunately, in our schooling. It has become a breeding ground for unconscious living.

Someone like me, a "good" student, was always used to asking for permission.

Raise your hand.

Sit quietly.

Complete all assignments.

I spent hours at night perfecting minute details in a project. Though many teachers called me a model student back then, the truth was I was just like every other kid in the class. I was motivated to make my parents proud of me and to set myself up for success. At least, this is what I thought I had to do to get rewarded.

Many times, our classroom management and reward systems confirm this for us. The golden star for the highest grade, the fake dollars when listening to the teacher, or the clip chart that slides from good to bad behavior. I believed if I did what was asked of me, the teacher would reward me. It's as if my self-worth had been monetized.

Was the education system actually supporting me as a person?

Or had I been put at the bottom of a mountain, learning to climb my way to the top?

Children are learning that in order to "Pass Go," you must listen silently, follow directions, and not question authority. Only then will you be rewarded and accepted. Thus, living an unconscious life.

So, how do we bring more consciousness, and thus conscious living, into our educational model?

When I spoke with Cara Planitz-Clatanoff, founder of Sabia Wisdom, she shared an analogy:

"Living a conscious life means seeing everything with new eyes. It means looking deeply at ourselves, how we've been conditioned to behave, and deciding for ourselves if that is the way we want to continue. It means opening our awareness to evaluate the world around us with a different perspective."

In order to see everything with new eyes, we need a new pair of glasses that clears our eyesight. We can then view how the rote mechanisms in our schooling lead to unconscious living in our adulthood. School teaches us to be unconscious by following what society tells us, which then feeds into our decision-making without really thinking about what we want.

How do we create this change of consciousness in the current model?

One way is through the practice of mindfulness and meditation. With almost ten times more children practicing meditation since 2012 (Centers for Disease Control and Prevention, 2019), this push has become more prevalent. The act of sitting down quietly and choosing to become aware of our inner world can be our first step. This allows children to sit with their thoughts and emotions, which reminds me of a classroom activity I used to do with my kids.

I would set up a table in the corner with various colors of loose glitter, a bulk set of Elmer's glue, and medium-sized Mason jars. Each of my students ran over excitingly and picked out their favorite colors. The activity was simple: warm up the water in the jar, mix in the glue, and add the glitter. *Stir, stir, stir, and shake.* As the jar shakes, the glitter floats around. But over time, the glitter settles down. This glitter represents our thoughts.

Our thoughts can settle down once you take a pause and breathe.

According to research done by Mindful Schools in 2019, students and teachers who practice mindfulness have heightened emotional regulation, which creates a number of changes in the brain that correspond to less reactivity. There is also a reduction of stress and feelings of anxiety, something we identified as major factors in the mental health crisis amongst children.

Mary Kayhoe, a mindfulness interventionist and Positive Behavior Intervention (PBS) coach, spoke to me about how mindfulness practices shifted the culture of her school that had 1,200 referrals. In her eyes, it was out of control.

"Kids were up in the hallway, missing a ton of instructional time. Even the discipline issues would take away from instructional time. [It was then I realized] the number of things that [the students] needed because they're not okay."

She realized the students struggled to understand their emotions and reactivity. After bringing mindfulness to both the staff and students, she decided to create a curriculum centered on these tools. Now, the students at the school are broken up into tiers based on their needs, and every child gets space to work on these conscious practices.

"The meditation part really helps to empower our students. [I always tell the students that] these are the times in school that you're here, and we want you to be here with us."

Certain lessons are powerful because they allow a child to learn about themselves. The whole child is being acknowledged as a human being, not just another troubled student. Not only that, but the child is also given the opportunity to return to the present moment and to move away from the constant need to strive.

When we decide to live more consciously, deeper questions emerge, such as:
- How are we conditioning children to become adults who are disconnected from their true selves?
- How are we disempowering children from living a life real to who they are?
- How are we teaching children that our external world is a place of validation?

To move from unconscious to conscious living, we must become aware.

"To become conscious is to become aware that in every moment, you are bringing an emotional legacy, emotional feeling, emotional touch, taste" -Shefali Tsabury ("How Consciousness Can Transform Education," 2019).

This comes into play as stakeholders (parents, teachers, educational leaders) in the schooling system. Are we willing to become aware of our own unconscious way of living? Are we willing to notice if we are the ones stuck on autopilot and how it is affecting our mental and spiritual health? We may not question what is causing this pain until we are willing to wake up. If we don't, our children will copy our behavior and pass unconscious habits down to other generations.

Our children deserve to be in tune with their consciousness and to connect *both* their internal and external worlds. When they are given the time and space to notice and build awareness, it cultivates a life of fulfillment.

Only with consciousness can our children create a life for themselves true to who they really are and contribute to the world at large.

11

LOOKING IN
THE MIRROR

———

*"We cannot change what we are not aware of, and once we
are aware, we cannot help but change."*

-SHERYL SANDBERG

I want you to do something for me: think about your favorite
teacher from school. Who had the biggest impact?

Chances are good that your answer falls into one of two cate-
gories. Some people can answer this question easily, responding with fond memories of their favorite instructor from their
formative years, while many others struggle to think of a
single person from their school years that they felt close to.

If you fall into the latter, you may have remembered someone,
but they weren't your favorite. Maybe, instead, it was the
teacher who had a negative impact on you; the unconscious
one that did more harm than good.

Chris McNutt, the founder of the Human Restoration Project, recalls a time when he was a "nerdy" eighth grader attending his social studies class. The teacher was ex-military; the sergeant in the room. Students were met with his daily lectures, delivered behind a large, wooden podium. The expectation was crystalized silence when he taught a lesson. He was the "original" schoolhouse teacher.

One day, McNutt and his classmates were working diligently on a group project, but one of the members wasn't present. Since the rest of the group had completed their tasks, the others decided to take a break. McNutt was a "model" student at the time and popped open a book quietly in the corner. When his teacher glanced over to see one of his exemplary students "slacking" off, he snapped.

An eraser flew against the whiteboard and the board fell off the wall.

Boom. The class gasped.

In the aftermath, Chris was assigned detention. Suddenly, in that moment, he learned he could do everything right but still be seen as wrong, and it shattered his sense of self and purpose.

His story showcases how one encounter with an unconscious teacher can lead to a lifelong mistrust of learning.

With so many children, both young and old, maintaining the wounds of broken consciousness, we need not only to help heal but to move forward. For too long, the hot shower has been fogging up the bathroom mirror, and it's time to bring a towel and wipe it clean.

Greater Good in Education, who researches science-based practices for kinder, happier schools, defines self-awareness as "the ability to be aware of one's inner life—one's emotions, thoughts, behaviors, values, mindsets...and how these elements impact behavior and choices," ("SEL for Adults: Self-Awareness and Self-Management," n.d.). It's a key step towards living a conscious life.

It begins with modeling it yourself.

This is what happened by my fifth year of teaching. Every day, the projector would pop up a slide with the words, "How are you feeling?" Each colorful character from Pixar's movie *Inside Out* was displayed on the screen: sadness, anger, fear, disgust, and joy. My students would immediately turn towards their "elbow" partner and share their feelings. A small chime would ring, and all eyes would close for a few minutes to breathe. Only then would the lesson begin.

Every time a student entered the classroom, this was the primary way they were greeted. Even when math lessons were being taught, my students knew their emotional and mental well-being was the foundation to learning math. But for the first four years of my teaching, I never integrated this into the classroom.

How could I share about emotional and mental well-being in a conscious manner when I hadn't done the work myself? As I felt more confident in my process to unlearn and relearn, I knew I was ready to share this process with my students.

It started with me.

It wasn't an easy journey. Ever since the death of my student, I had to shine a light into every dark crevice to find those unconscious parts of myself. I understood that I was part of the problem and not the solution. Even if I thought I was an effective teacher, my guidance was still layered with conditioning in my mind, pushing external benchmarks that did not fit the needs of my students. And, as always, this process of self-awareness came with discomfort.

When we sit with parts of ourselves, it means we may have to confront things most of us are conditioned to avoid and suppress. Many times, it's our uncomfortable emotions that take a back seat. I'm not sure about you, but as someone who struggles with her own emotions, I catch myself scrolling through my phone, watching the next binge-worthy Netflix show, or eating my favorite carrot cake. These are all distractions.

Though this avoidance makes me feel safe temporarily, I evade looking deeper at the wound. Without this awareness, we are unable to reach our highest potential. Motivational speaker, Tony Robbins, shares, "Self-awareness is one of the rarest of human commodities. When you become aware of your own patterns—when you know why you are the way you are—you can finally begin to be honest with yourself," (Robbins, 2021).

This goes for every single stakeholder in the educational model, including parents, teachers, leaders, and students. In particular, educators and students benefit from this active process. According to CASEL, shared in an earlier chapter, children and adults need to have self-awareness to understand emotions, feel and show empathy, and maintain positive relationships ("SEL for Adults: Self-Awareness and Self-Management," n.d.). In order to be of service to children, we must be of service to ourselves.

Educators who focus on this portion of their lives may be favored to less burnout and turnover. This leads to more positive emotions, thus better relationships with students. It's like an air bag falling from overhead on a plane. In order to help someone else, you need to have oxygen first. This is all part of bringing consciousness into our lives through deeper awareness. It starts with looking inward.

When all individuals within the education system begin to question themselves, there is room to pinpoint when we are emotionally reactive, and from where it stems. Many times, I was unaware of my impact on children within my own classroom. When I reflected, I uncovered some hard truths. It was like peeling back an onion.

The self-awareness and reflection process is a personal one, and there are ways to begin no matter who you are. Even if it feels like the tip of the iceberg, it's a starting point. Here are some helpful ways to begin:

1. Label and recognize one's emotions. Remember your first day of school when you walked into that new classroom, filled with nervous butterflies? There was excitement bubbling up in your stomach, knowing you were about to meet new friends and a new teacher? Well, in that very moment, you navigated your own inner world, realizing your emotional triggers and learning how to work through them the best way you could.

For many of us, the way we navigate our emotions comes from the messaging we got growing up. What comes up for you when you hear the word emotion? Maybe it's weakness or vulnerability? Or maybe it's strength? This baggage starts in our childhood and gets carried with us into adulthood. Until we understand how to become self-aware of our own emotions, we will continue to become reactive to the environments our children stand in.

Here are some questions to get you started:

What is my relationship with my emotions? Do I feel them enough or do I repress them?

Do I believe there are bad and good emotions? How do I share emotions with children?

Am I comfortable talking about emotions? If not, how is the best way to do so?

Once we create a personal relationship with our emotions, we are better equipped to identify our triggers from the past.

This then promotes more consciousness in spaces with others, giving children permission to feel everything as well.

2. Unlearn one's judgments and biases. Most of the time, certain judgments and biases are unconscious. According to the Office of Diversity and Outreach, unconscious biases are "social stereotypes about certain groups of people that individuals form outside their own conscious awareness...these biases stem from one's tendency to organize social worlds by categorizing," (UCSF, 2016).

These unconscious biases are just that: unconscious. They become entrenched in our thought patterns. When I became a teacher, I had to face many of these implicit biases. For example, I realized I treated boys and girls differently. I didn't even know I was doing it until I started witnessing the following:

- I always liked the girls who were not as outspoken and quietly listened at their desks (like myself growing up).
- I always told the girls they were "beautiful" and "kind."
- I always asked the boys to help push desks or pick up heavy boxes.

For me, it was an extremely uncomfortable moment to realize my own implicit biases after years of teaching. Yet, once I named it, I decided to make a conscious shift to be more inclusive with my students. Here are some questions to unpack:

Which groups of people did I get positive messages about growing up?

Which groups of people did I get negative messages about growing up?

Have I actively tried to change this? How may this be passed down onto children?

3. Understand the relationship between one's emotions, thoughts, and behaviors. Our inner world is complex. Our thought patterns make us feel a certain way, and ultimately, dictate how we act. It's like when you watch the news and see a local murder. Someone usually has a visceral reaction, whether it is anger towards the killer or empathy for the victim's family. This fear can lead to frustration for the rest of the day. Just like this automatic response, we live in a fast-paced world without frequent pauses. When we do pause, however, we can ask some questions like:

What are the repeated thought patterns I have? (Ex. I'm not good enough, life is hard, people are not to be trusted, etc.)

Do I treat myself with compassion or am I very hard on myself?

How do my fears affect the way I show up every day?

When I spoke with Dido Balla, the director of Educational Innovation and Partnerships at the non-profit MindUp, he shared how adults hated him when he was a kid since he asked too many questions. When he became a teacher and kids asked him those same questions, it triggered him.

"It was an opportunity for me to explore and look into what it looks like to be frustrated."

This ability to be mindful can cultivate more conscious interactions with children.

4. Intentionally build one's relationships. No matter what kind of relationship we have in our lives, from friendship to romantic, it takes effort; however, the greatest amount of work is the relationship with self. Yet, it's only with that warm bath at night or relaxing with some board games that we find a space for self-compassion. When we don't fill our cups first, we could have a bad day and project our feelings onto someone else—especially children. This means it takes awareness to see how we build and maintain relationships.

What types of people do you have a good relationship with?

What types of people trigger you? How do they trigger you? Who do they remind you of?

How do you form authentic relationships with children? How is your relationship with yourself?

It's easy to become critical when self-reflecting, but it can open up so many doors. When we actively notice our inner world, we move toward consciousness. This awareness can create more conscious spaces in the educational model. Until we conquer this consciousness, we will continue to struggle to support future students.

I spoke with Julia Fliss, an educator of over twenty years, who went through deep self-awareness and reflection to become a conscious educator herself. Fliss is a passionate language arts teacher from Evergreen Middle School and speaks to how she shifted the paradigm of her role as a teacher. Her philosophy is to be a lifelong learner and engage with her students in a way that creates community in the classroom.

She begins the school year asking questions to her students, such as:

"What do you need to learn and what do you want to learn?"

"How can you connect with what's going on around us?"

"What do you see around you that you would like to know more about?"

She integrates a project-based approach in the classroom, enabling students to utilize projects to link their learning from inside the classroom to outside of the classroom, and vice versa.

"I feel like I'm a facilitator. I am the connector in the classroom between the learning and our experiences of it. The learning doesn't come from me. I bring in the resources, modes of understanding, and areas of study. But truly, it's the kids who share the learning. I learn more from them."

However, this perspective didn't come right away. It came from years of unconscious experiences where Fliss realized she needed to wake up to a new way of learning.

"I did not want to live my life with my eyeballs in a book [while pursuing pre-med]. I was looking for the information, and then I realized that it's not in a book, and it's not in a grade. It's not in the way you look or something outside of you, but it's in yourself."

Now, Julia is a Sustainable Development Goals (SDG) ambassador, empowering her students to engage with their own community as well as the world at large. When I spoke with her via video call, her classroom was blanketed with large colorful posters hanging on the walls displaying student work, images of the universe covering the ceiling to remind students of their worldly connection, and community agreements representing a culture of unity.

Fliss is a classic example of how her own personal development resulted in the conscious space she created for her students. Self-awareness and self-reflection are the first steps toward consciousness in the educational system. It's here we can cultivate individuals who are committed to becoming conscious of themselves, giving children the chance to do the same.

Every adult can finally move from sage on the stage to the guide on the side.

12

THE NEW GROWTH MINDSET

———

*"Progress is impossible without change, and those who can-
not change their minds cannot change anything."*

-GEORGE BERNARD SHAW

"I want you to think of every failure that you've had. Every
teacher that told you that you couldn't do it. Every teacher
that told you that you weren't good at math. And I want you
to feel that anger while you throw this paper ball against
the wall."

My students stare ahead at the whiteboard, trembling with
anticipation as they clutch their paper balls tightly. Their
dormant anger is pulsating through their veins.

I know I hit a nerve.

"All right...one, two, three!"

All twenty-eight-paper balls shoot through the air, hitting the whiteboard.

Sighs of relief echo in the room.

This is the start of a new mindset.

Every year, I started my growth mindset lesson with a paper ball. By the time my students reached sixth grade, they had already been through at least seven years of schooling. In this short time, I knew that unconscious damage had been done. It was evident when young boys and girls would sit, fists clenched to their paper balls, recalling every moment they didn't believe in themselves. Or worse, someone else that didn't. The damage had been done.

It represented everything wrong with our educational model.

I was always prepared to encounter students who had a strong belief of what their role was within the school system; the same boxes of "good" or "bad" that have been mentioned earlier. Mind you, I don't mean the actual capabilities of a child, but rather how adults in the space and the system perceived them.

It was as if failure had become part of their DNA.

Every mistake in their learning made a child feel as if they were not "good enough." Every score on a test proved it. Thus, some students didn't believe they were smart. This became even worse with the horror that is math, a subject that brought shivers down my students' spines. Math was rigid. It was structured and always had a right answer.

Even parents I encountered had their own self-limiting beliefs about their math capabilities.

"I was never good at math growing up."

"My child won't be good at math because I never was."

So how would I combat this? I discovered Carol Dweck's work in *Mindset: The New Psychology of Success.*

In Dweck's research, she tried to evaluate how implicit beliefs influence one's identity. She explored two theories: *fixed mindset vs. growth mindset.* Fixed mindset is the belief that your intelligence can't be changed, as if you are born with your full potential. On the other hand, a growth mindset is the idea that your talents and abilities can be developed; just like riding a bike or a baby learning to walk. With consistency, the neurons in our brains can create deeper connections. This leads to learning and growth.

"...[O]ur studies show that teaching people to have a 'growth mindset' encourages a focus on effort rather than on intelligence or talent, and helps make them into high achievers in school and in life," (Dweck, 2007).

Since I taught ten-year-old students with highly malleable brains, I knew this mindset could be utilized for learning in school. I still had a chance to shift their personal beliefs about this so-called "dreadful" subject. Therefore, the paper ball experiment did wonders.

As the balls fly, students scream and jump up. There is a rush of excitement. Each student runs to pick up a mashed paper ball and carefully opens it. Their eyes light up as they run back to their seats. It is here I pause.

"Each crinkle in the paper is a representation of a neuron in your brain. Every 'failure' or 'mistake' you've made in the classroom was not bad, it actually helped your brain grow."

The students look at me with wide eyes. This one statement goes against everything they believe about themselves. This is the first time they correlate mistakes with learning. With hesitation, they open the caps of markers, coloring in each wrinkle, or neuron. Within seconds, their chests puff up and they are filled with pride.

Year after year, this activity did wonders. It was the seed planted and watered daily. It resulted in a strong culture of growth mindset. I saw students challenging their embedded beliefs, realizing they could be good at any subject. Yes, even math.

They would excitingly share.

"It's okay I made a mistake. I just grew my brain."

"I'll try to do the challenge problem. It's okay if I get it wrong."

"Ms. Shah, I used to hate math. But now I love it. I might just be good at it."

This was music to my ears. But then again, there was a simultaneous knot in my stomach. Here I was, creating a culture of progress, growth, and celebrating mistakes; yet, every time I did this activity, it felt like something was not right. The mindset shift I was advocating for was trying to undo the damage already done.

I shouldn't have to be this reactive. This lesson was a short-term fix to a long-term problem. It felt like the baby rescue operation had come back again. The long-term problem was the education system itself, only rewarding the students who kept up with the predetermined pace. It was a system that applauded memorization over the ebbs and flows of the learning process.

How had I become so entrenched in this problem?

I taught growth mindset to my students, but the same message kept ringing in my head:

Good grades.

Good college.

Good job.

It was then I realized I had forgotten how to use a growth mindset not just for myself, but also for the system itself.

The question becomes: *why are we so resistant to growth?*

Our brains like certainty, as supported by the NeuroLeadership Institute. In order to survive, we want to control the outcome. This becomes counterintuitive when we experience change. Our brains see it as a "threat" or a "challenge." The former leads to distress, and the latter leads to eustress: *a positive response.* In order to perceive change as a challenge, and still within your capabilities, it involves developing that growth mindset. Whether you are a parent, educator, or a change maker, implementing these daily steps for education leads to growth. Here are some suggestions: (Derler and Ray, 2019)

1. Reframe your thinking to view change as a challenge, not as a threat. It's okay to become fearful of change in the educational model, but can we see it as something positive? Instead of seeing it as dismantling a structure that once worked, can we be open-minded to innovation?

2. Celebrate moments of progress during the change. Every step toward consciousness is a celebratory moment. Even if the progress feels small, it is still making an impact.

3. Give yourself permission to start experimenting along the way. This is not all or nothing. It's a step toward betterment for all children.

4. Learn from peers who seem to model the growth mindset well. Every stakeholder within the educational system pushing for change is someone to admire. They have the perspective of growth, rather than stagnation.

5. Look for ways to lead by example, even if you aren't always confident. There is no right or wrong. Just as we develop this awareness for children, we also allow that for ourselves. Self-compassion is key.

I bring these strategies up because it gives us a place to start to change how we perceive education as a whole, knowing the inevitable resistance accompanying it. It's also asking a key question:

What is the purpose of education?

As Jay Shetty, a former monk and now acclaimed motivational speaker, shares, "The purpose of education is to help someone get as close to their truest identity as possible. [It's] beyond the physical, mental, and emotional understanding of the self," (Campbell, 2018).

This takes a mindset shift. More often than not, our history suggests that education is built to ensure a bright future for a child. Yet, this has become in accordance with standardization and moved away from a child's unique path and how to learn in their truest manner.

So, if we did use this definition, how would our education look?

In early childhood education, individualized spaces are created to give children time to explore their curiosity. This could be through play-based learning with art and outdoor activities, as well as inquiry-based work, as seen with Montessori schools. Children would also be exposed to consciousness exercises like mindfulness to introduce the inner world. We would move away from focusing primarily on academics and instead cultivate the natural qualities that lie in every child.

When this type of consciousness comes into school spaces, it makes children feel seen and heard. The focus on the inner world is a mindset shift for us all. It's not how we have been conditioned for what success looks like, but it is still necessary. I had the privilege to speak to two educators who have transformed their style based on consciousness.

JG Larochette, the founder of Mindful Life Project, had been a long-term elementary school teacher in his local community. Larochette worked tirelessly to support children emotionally and academically, but he lost himself in the process. It led to a breakdown.

In order to cope, Larochette sought out intervention methods. He was out of luck until one day he found it: mindfulness. For a full year, Larochette self-reflected, unlearned, and tried to relearn a new mindset. His students were patient with his transformation, and one day he decided to share this gift with his third graders. He nervously stood in a packed classroom of twenty-five kids and began to introduce this practice.

Initially, he thought there would be no change. Teaching eight-year-olds to sit silently for fifteen seconds seemed like a long shot, but he described the moment he saw his kids become quiet for the very first time.

"These kids, all of them had gotten quiet, and all of them closed their eyes, which was already a win for me. They were all supposed to go for two minutes...and literally after two minutes, I could see everyone was still quiet. All eyes were still closed."

Larochette was shocked. He thought his students were messing with him; however, the energy in the room was relaxed. When his students opened their eyes, there was a sense of calm in the room. It was at this moment that Larochette saw the impact of mindfulness with children. His students exclaimed:

"That's the most peaceful I've felt."

"That was the calmest I felt."

"I was floating in the clouds."

Larochette wasn't sure if this would last forever. It wasn't until he ran into two of his students doing a mindful sit during recess. These were the same girls who had been fighting in his classroom a few minutes before. Larochette finally saw its possibilities. It was the first step towards consciousness, but not the last. JG's journey led him on a mission to integrate mindfulness into the classroom. He broadened his impact, serving 10,300 students at twenty-two underserved schools. He has utilized this work to support educators in their own practice of mindfulness.

I spoke with another teacher, Nicole Vetere, the founder of New Age Teacher and an educator for twenty-plus years in Canada. Vetere shared how stifled she felt in school growing up and how she wanted to do better for her students.

"Some teachers that I had really squashed creativity [when I was young]. I think it's this whole being in the box thing. And I just knew that we [children] were meant to be creators.

We are creative innately and I wanted to keep that alive for kids. I wanted them to know how to use their gifts and share it with the world."

Vetere first introduced simple meditations to her kids and noticed the shift in her classroom. The students began to use incredible language that most kids don't use every day. They showed up differently for writing or the way they solved a problem, but this wasn't the only impact. Her consciousness focus in the classroom shifted for parents as well.

"Parents [were] coming in for interviews and speaking to it...I've had parents say, 'my kids come home and teach me everything you're teaching them.' It's just the greatest gift because many of their parents haven't been on this journey and some of them have been introduced to this journey, just from what their kids are bringing home and teaching them."

After Vetere's shift in her mindset as an educator, she's realized the truest potential of her students. "When you open up that space and you hold space for them, it's incredible. They're so intuitive and their spirit is so large, but they just need the space to be in it, to feel safe to expose that part of themselves to us."

These are just flowers in a bigger garden. With a growth mindset ourselves, we shift the educational system and transform it toward something better. When we do this, our mindset shifts an outdated paradigm focusing on externalized success. We can build a new vision where children will be nurtured to live exponentially healthier and happier lives.

This, ultimately, can reshape the world as we see it.

In Carol Dweck's words, "Change can be tough, but I've never heard anybody say it wasn't worth it," (Dweck, 2007).

CONCLUSION

A CONSCIOUS REVOLUTION

———

A child leaving the education system as a mindful, connected, fulfilled young adult.

This is my hope.

At the beginning of my fifth year of teaching, I gave my classroom a much-needed makeover. Though I spent hours browsing Pinterest for picture-perfect classroom decor, none of the classrooms really spoke to me. Though they were beautiful, they felt just like mine—colorful but cold. I needed something different, so that summer, I snatched our school's roll of yellow butcher paper and plastered it over one of the walls in my classroom. It was happy and bright, lending a warm glow to the rest of my room. But something was missing.

As I stared at the wall, I realized what it needed...and I started writing. I covered that paper with inspirational quotes, mantras, and caricatures of emotions; some of the many ways I knew consciousness could be symbolized. Then, in big, bold letters, I wrote in the center, "How Are You Feeling?" I wanted this wall to speak to children who walked into my classroom, to tell them they were seen, heard, and loved. I wanted to start a revolution.

And I did for some time. Though I tried hard, I came to the harder realization that a revolution couldn't sustain itself within the confines of a classroom. I was just a small fish in a big pond. Instead, I had to go beyond my immediate control and focus on something greater and scarier—the system at large.

This is the same system that for so long had treated its children as if they need to fit the worn-down fabric instead of sewing something new. This was for every individual whose message had been slightly different and had been ostracized by a model whose values were external benchmarks and "one size fits all."

I realize this work is not a one-woman show, but instead a collaboration of each and every one of us stakeholders' part of this educational model.

The school leader frustrated with the systems and policies.

The educator overwhelmed by the pressure of standards and lesson plans.

The parents hopeless in seeing their child lose their love of learning.

The former student whose true nature was never cultivated.

Each one of us creates pieces of the whole puzzle. And we have one common mission: to do better than those before. To create an educational system that supports and nurtures all children.

It's going to take a village where every member believes a new system is possible.

An education system cultivating the future generations with children at the heart.

An education system creating spaces for children to explore and express their emotions and to seek help when they are in trouble.

An education system teaching children to become strong and confident self-advocates.

An education system fostering strong, healthy relationships between teachers and students.

An education system cultivating self-worth based on whom you are, not what you become.

Transforming our educational system can no longer be an impossible feat. We must do what we can now to change our schools for the better. We must be willing to give children futures they deserve.

"Our children are the rock on which our future will be built, our greatest asset as a nation." - Nelson Mandela (Detoro, 2018).

Collectively, we have a chance to uplift many generations to come. Each one of us has the power and ability to create a system that is not only healing but also inclusive of one's potential. It's a place where a child's inner world is seen as foundational for learning and, ultimately, life. This revolution starts with us, and it continues with our children.

Let's cultivate consciousness in education. It is time for a new legacy.

RAISING OUR HANDS

———

This vision is a collaborative effort. I have learned throughout this process that in order to bring consciousness into our educational spaces, it will take intentional and continued conversation about how we can do better for children—*all* children.

I invite you to join the *Raise Your Hand!* Facebook community where you can meet other passionate individuals and like-minded educators ready to ask the right questions to progress toward a new future.

I would love to connect with you further. You can find me at https://thekomalshah.com to learn more about my educational consulting services. I am always open to talk about how to bring consciousness into your school space, alternative space, or any other spaces needing this type of work.

This is a collective mission. I can't wait to see you there.

DISCUSSION GUIDE

———

This guide has been created as open-ended questions that will push you to reflect. The suggestion is to utilize this guide in two ways:

1) Reflect after reading each chapter, or

2) Finish the book and choose five to seven questions that personally resonate with you to reflect on either personally or in a group.

INTRODUCTION

1) The author starts the book with a story of her student passing away. What about this story resonated with you? Are there any parts that shook you?

2) The author shares "…[let's] build an educational system that focuses on children's inner self as opposed to their external, marketable success." What do you think she meant by that? Do you agree with this or not? Explain.

3) The author states, "It felt like their humanity had been stripped away from them in the name of learning." Did you ever experience having to be resilient in the classroom? If you are an educator, did you suppress emotions in the name of learning? Why do you think we should shift this?

CHAPTER 1

1) The author shares in detail the history of our educational system. Based on her research, which parts of the educational history shocked you? In what ways?

2) Which parts of our educational history still ring true today? How so?

3) Do you agree that our education system has failed to change? If so, why do you think so?

4) What do **you** think are the long-term effects of a factory and fear-based educational model?

CHAPTER 2

1) The author explores the definition of success. What messages were you given growing up about the idea of success? Do you agree with those same messages today?

2) The author shares, "We've been taught that success is outside of ourselves." Do you agree with this statement? Why or why not?

3) Within our education system, what messages of success do we communicate to students? In what ways? How should we change them?

CHAPTER 3

1) The author goes into a parable of babies falling into the river. What was your initial reaction to this parable? What do you think the author was trying to convey with this parable?

2) The author makes a bold point that the school system perpetuates the mental health crisis in our children. Do you agree with this? Why or why not?

3) It's stated that this is not a mental health crisis but a spiritual health crisis. Do you think that our school system is disconnecting students from who they are? If so, in what ways?

CHAPTER 4

1) The author shares her passion for dancing. Was there something that brought you joy growing up? Were you encouraged or discouraged to make it a career? What were the reasons that were given either way?

2) There is a focus on the mind-body-spirit connection of children. Play-based learning and mindfulness are described as possible modalities to cultivate this in children. What other methods or activities would you suggest? Why should we incorporate them and how?

CHAPTER 5

1) Unlearning is one of the most powerful ways to become conscious of ourselves. What are one or two examples of unlearning that you have achieved in your own life?

2) What unlearning do you think educators and leaders need to accomplish within our schools in order to better support students?

3) If time allows, answer the following questions that the author proposed regarding your own education:
- Did I like school growing up? Why or why not?
- What does success look like to me? How was it messaged to me?
- Are there harmful messages in school?
- Do I believe in the culture of achievement perpetuated in schools?
- Was I emotionally supported while being in school? If not, why not?

CHAPTER 6

1) Were you accepted for being your authentic self growing up? Name ways in which you were or were not. (For example, I was accepted for my joy but not my anger...)

2) The author asks, "What does it REALLY mean to be you?" Do you think this would be powerful to ask our students in the classroom? Why or why not?

CHAPTER 7

1) What messages did you receive growing up about emotions? Were you free to express them? How did you know?

2) The author shares how teachers also need to be supported emotionally in schools. What do you think this would look like?

3) How powerful do you feel it would be to support students emotionally? What are the barriers to incorporating this in schools? How do we overcome these barriers?

CHAPTER 8

1) The author shares a story about a student who is suffering trauma from his home life. Have you seen this with other students or children? Do you think schools are responsible to address this trauma? Why or why not?

2) There is a call to move away from a sole focus on academic learning to the whole child. In your opinion, how should we go about this?

CHAPTER 9

1) There is a call for self-care for educators in order to build relationships with students. What do you think are the barriers in terms of teachers and self-care? How can teachers be more supported in this area?

2) What can school administrators and leaders do to foster a better culture of rest and relaxation for the most vulnerable, teachers?

CHAPTER 10

1) Before you read this chapter, how did you define consciousness? Did your definition change after reading the chapter?

2) The author goes into detail about how living an unconscious life is described as being on autopilot. Did you or do you ever experience this in your own life? In what ways?

3) In what ways, in your opinion, is our educational system unconscious?

4) How are we teaching children that our external world is a place of validation? Do you still believe in this yourself?

CHAPTER 11

1) The author describes that the first step to becoming more conscious is self-awareness. Do you think this can actually lead to a more conscious education system? Why or why not?

2) The author goes into detail about various questions to ask yourself. Go back to the chapter starting on page 158 and answer two to three questions of your choice.

CHAPTER 12

1) Why do you think having a growth mindset is so powerful?

2) In what ways, in your opinion, can we show a growth mindset when it comes to the schooling system?

CONCLUSION

1) The author claims that a collaboration among all stakeholders in necessary to bring more consciousness into education. What advice would you give to each stakeholder?

2) The author makes the following claims. Which one resonates with you and why?

- An education system cultivating the future generation with children at the heart.
- An education system creating spaces for children to explore and express their emotions and to seek help when they are in trouble.
- An education system teaching children to become strong and confident self-advocates.
- An education system fostering strong, healthy relationships between teachers and students.
- An education system cultivating self-worth based on who you are, not what you become.

FINAL QUESTION

What is your role, and how can you bring more consciousness to yourself and the system as a whole? Write down three ways in which you hope to contribute to this conscious revolution. What would be your first step?

ACKNOWLEDGMENTS

———

If you had asked me a year ago if I would be writing a book, let alone one on my vision for education, I would have laughed in disbelief; however, when the pandemic hit, I decided to take the uncertainty of my life and pour some fuel into something I had dreamt of for so long. Now I sit here and reflect on the people that supported me every step of the way. It truly has taken a village.

I have to start by thanking my family. To my mom and dad, Sangita and Tushar, thank you for housing and nurturing me throughout this process. You welcomed me with open arms after moving home after eleven years. You have become my pillars during this time, always cheering me on from the sidelines. I am indebted to you. To my brother Pritesh, and one of my biggest inspirations, thank you for always believing in my dreams, and validating that I have something to share with the world.

I have to give a heartfelt thank you to one of my dearest friends, Sarah Daniels. You truly are my *dream defender*. Thank you for choosing to sit with me every week to create a vision board of my new life. You showed me what was possible and gave me the courage to create a future in alignment with my greatest self. I value your heart and your love for others. I am so lucky to have you in my life.

A big thank you to my six beta readers: Dr. Stacey Gonzales, Dr. Dawn DiPeri, Fabienne Vailes, Janet Wi, Josie Innamorato, and Julia Fliss. You all took time out of your busy schedules to read my entire manuscript from front to back and provide me thoughtful feedback. Thank you for your willingness to support my journey. I want to give a special shout-out to Cara Planitz-Clatanoff for taking the time to bring my words to life. You have shown me the dearest friendship.

A special thank you to my fellow crew of authors: Ester Teper, Ethan Turner, Mohamad Yassin, and Sasi Yajamanyam. I wouldn't have survived this process without our many Zoom calls and co-writing sessions. I have to give a much-needed shout-out to Ethan for being my writing buddy for the last two months during the revisions process and giving me both pep talks and accountability as we pushed toward the finish line.

When I decided to write this book, the education community and their unconditional support of my endeavors shocked me. I want to thank the over seventy educators I had the privilege to interview. Though I am unable to name you all, you know who you are. Each one of you inspires me and gives me faith with your relentless dedication to do better for children.

None of this would have been possible without Eric Koester and the Creator Institute. I still remember jumping on a phone call to share my initial book idea. Within a month, I had joined a program that would change my life forever. Eric, your vision has shifted the lives of so many. Thank you to my publisher, New Degree Press, and my publishing team. To my developmental editor, Kyrsten Rice, I am the writer I am today because of you. Thank you for pushing me to break down my ideas, and for showing me that my vision is possible. To my marketing and revisions editor, Kathy Wood, thank you for holding my hand throughout the process, giving me grace when needed, and healing me with your words.

Lastly, thank you to all my students. I am here today because of you. You changed my life by giving me a new perspective on the potential of every child. I wake up every morning with every one of you in my heart. Without you, none of this would have been possible. Sincerely, Ms. Shah.

Here are the names of all those who contributed to my pre-launch campaign. You are deeply appreciated for helping make this book a reality:

Aaron Berman	Alison Sullivan
Aarthi Ajit	Alli Jaeggi
Aarti Patel	Amanda Bennett
Aasna J Shah	Amanjot Singh
Adi Manvich	Amit Kapadia
Ajouni Singh	Amy DeLair
Akhil Sud	Andrew McLoon
Alex Pham	Anna McVeigh-Murphy
Alexander Peiffer	Anne Ziemniak
Ali Stewart	Apurva Shroff
Ali Wallace	Armughan Syed
Alicia Del Fierro	Arti Mehta
Alie Kelley	Arti Sheth

Arvind R Nagarajan

Asavari Bhogle

Ashley Rodriguez

Avantika Singh

Avi Soor

Azim Hirani

Belal Breaga Bakht

Beth Salyers

Bharat Shah

Bhavesh Sheth

Bhavini Purohit

Bridgette Love

Brionna DeVos

Bushra Khan

Caitlin Shelburne

Candace Bribiesca

Cara Planitz- Clatanoff

Carlo Mahfouz

Cassidy Younghans

Cecile Aguillaume

Chandni Shah

Chhaya Samtani

Chirag Shah

Chris Clay

Chris Cronin

Chris Ouayoro

Christopher Chiang

Colleen Mallen

Corey Esquivias

Courtney Guenard

Courtney Zhang

Daniel Patrick Dolan

Daphne Jones

Darby Rousseau

Darcie Odom

Dave Banse

Desmond Dunham

Destiny Davis

Dinesh Gurupur

Dipak Mody

Dipesh Shah

Divya Unni

Dominic Strezynski

Donae Fourth

Dorothy Dai

Dr Chandrakant V Shah

Dr. Trudi Lynne Perkins

Drasti Mody

Ebenezer Gyasi

Ekansh Gupta

Elizabeth Orona

Elizabeth Pinborough

Elizabeth Prather

Emily Delaplaine

Emily Sampson

Eric Koester

Evelyn Brill

Farhana Lubna

Farrell Murphy
Felix Dey
Frederick Keith II
Gayathri Dravid
Gustavo De Paz
Hafiza Stratton
Harita Patel
Harsha Sheth
Hashruti Amin
Heather Cowap
Helen Guan
Hetvi Bhagat
Hillary Schoelzel
Holly Marie Owens
Imani Moody
Ishika Seth
Jacob Leonard
Janet Wi
Jason Lau
Jatin Kadakia
Jatin Patel
Jenny Ham
Jenny Shah
Jessica Holcombe
Jessica Hong
Jessica Liu
Jignesh Shah
Joanna Koss
Joel Anttumalil
John Lehoczky
Jonathan Crane
Jordan Staenberg

Joshua David
Justin Gordon
Justine Laporte
Jyoti Parekh
Jyotika Soni
Kacper Kruszewski
Karen Romero
Karishma Chauhan
Kassandre A Harper-Cotton
Katelin Stidham
Katherine Conover
Kathir Palaniyappan
Kelsey Navis
Ketul Patel
Kevin Fohrer
Krish Kumar
Kyoko Utsumi
LaNysha Adams
LaShante Smith
Laura Chesney
Laura Gardiner
Laura Tippett
Lauren Krasnodembski
Leiana Swanson
Lillian Roselin
Lindsay Chiccone
Lynn Rosenblatt
Madeleine Olson
Madison Baker
Maggie Favretti
Manish Shah
Marusya Price

Maryam Garg
Matt Andersen
Matthew Barnes
Megan Macpherson
Melinda Casey
Micah Stilwell
Michael Small
Michelle Jones
Mike Gullo
Mike Yates
Mohit Gupta
Mona Sampath
Monali Varaiya
Morten Relster
Nadine Wilches
Najee Boucher
Namita Varaiya
Nanddas Bambhania
Nathan Ross
Neha Shah
Nell Derick Debevoise
Nick Barnett
Nicole Vetere
Nikitha Reddy
Nimish Dave
Nyle Rioux
Paaras Mehta
Pai-Ling Yin
Parag Mehta
Parin Patel
Parnika Singh
Parool Modi

Parul Khandeshi
Parul Kothari
Parul Shah
Patty Suquilanda
Payal Sud
Piyush Patel
Pooja Klebig
Pooja Parashar
Prafulla Soni
Pranav Tadi
Pranoy Rodrigues
Prapti Patel
Prashant Shah
Premlata Hazariwala
Pritesh Shah
Priyanka Anandampillai
Priyanka Karande
Purva Lad
Quinn Tempest
Radhika Bahl
Raksha Raghunath
Ramesh Rakholia
Ravi Patel
Rebecca von dem Hagen
Rekha Savla
Richard McCrow
Richard Russell
Riddhi Lunkad
Robert Smith
Roger Osorio
Roshni Kakiya
Ryan Jach

Sachin Shah
Saloni Soni
Samir Mehta
Sandra Guindi
Sapna Khandwala
Sarah Daniels
Sarah Rothenberg
Sarah Rotterman
Scott Van Beck
Seth Fleischauer
Shalaka Prabhune
Shalini Garg
Shane P Durkan
Shannon Stewart
Shefali Shah
Sherif Saadawi
Shilpan Sheth
Shivam Patel
Shruti Dhingra
Sierra Gomez
Simeen Shaikh
Skylar Primm
Social Upheaval
Stas Arsonov

Stefanie Cohen
Steve Manney
Suh-Pyng Ku
Suma Shivaprasad
Sumhita Anant
Sur Samtani
Sweta Kadakia
Taylor Haar
Tela Caul
Teri-Cole Smith
Thomas Yoon
Tim O' Hara
Tina Diaz
Traci N. Smith
Trevor Rosenbery
Tushar Shah
Tyler Atwood
Umang Mehta
Veena Agnihotri
Victor Gonzalez
Vidhi Kantawala
Vishal Patel
Wendy Weeks
Zoe Weil

APPENDIX

———

CHAPTER 1

Clifton, Jim. "The World's Broken Workplace." *The Chairman's Blog* (blog). June 13, 2017. https://news.gallup.com/opinion/chairman/212045/world-broken-workplace.aspx?g_source=position1&g_medium=related&g_campaign=tiles.

"Fight or Flight Response." Psychology Tools. 2021. https://www.psychologytools.com/resource/fight-or-flight-response/#:~:text=Information%20Handout.

Forbes. "The History of Education." November 1, 2012. Video, 11:27. https://www.youtube.com/watch?v=LqTwDDTjb6g.

Freedom in Thought. "How to Create an Absolutely Broken School System." September 5, 2017. Video, 5:30. https://www.freedominthought.com/archive/why-is-the-school-system-failing-the-future-of-education.

McLeod, Saul. "What Is Conformity? | Simply Psychology." Simply Psychology. 2018. https://www.simplypsychology.org/asch-conformity.html.

Sadhguru. "Watch Sadhguru's Experience of Education with CEO of EduComp." February 14, 2013. Video, 8:42. https://www.youtube.com/watch?time_continue=1&v=Ey24zdSY84A&feature=emb_logo.

TED. "Do Schools Kill Creativity? | Sir Ken Robinson." January 6, 2007. Video, 20:03. https://www.youtube.com/watch?v=iG9CE55wbtY&t=1s.

The Film Archives. "Education Is a System of Indoctrination of the Young— Noam Chomsky." June 1, 2012. Video, 7:35. https://www.youtube.com/watch?v=JVqMAlgAnlo.

Valencia, Nicolás. "The Same People Who Designed Prisons Also Designed Schools." *Arch Daily.* May 19, 2020. https://www.archdaily.com/905379/the-same-people-who-designed-prisons-also-designed-schools.

"Why Is the School System Failing? The Future of Education." *Freedom in Thought (blog).* August 28, 2017. https://www.freedominthought.com/archive/why-is-the-school-system-failing-the-future-of-education.

Zinkina, Julia, Andrey Korotayev, and Alexey I. Andreev. "Mass Primary Education in the Nineteenth Century." Uchitel Publishing House. 2013. https://www.sociostudies.org/almanac/articles/mass_primary_education_in_the_nineteenth_century/.

CHAPTER 2

Adkins, Amy. "What Millennials Want from Work and Life." *Gallup Workplace (blog).* May 10, 2016. https://www.gallup.com/workplace/236477/millennials-work-life.aspx.

Chui, Anna. "Why People Who Succeed at School Don't Always Succeed in Life." *Lifehack (blog).* 2021. https://www.lifehack.org/560957/success-school-doesnt-equal-success-life.

Curwin, Richard. "Six Reasons Rewards Don't Work." *Edutopia (blog).* March 6, 2012. https://www.edutopia.org/blog/reward-fraud-richard-curwin.

Ruth, Angela. "Thomas Edison—10,000 Ways That Won't Work." *Due* (blog). August 22, 2016. https://due.com/blog/thomas-edison-10000-ways-that-wont-work/.

Schoeffel, Mark, Peter Kuriloff, and Margaret van Steenwyk. "NAIS—How Do You Define Success?" National Association of Independent Schools. Summer 2011. https://www.nais.org/magazine/independent-school/summer-2011/how-do-you-define-success/.

CHAPTER 3

Abeles, Vicki, Grace Rubenstein, and Lynda Weinman. *Beyond Measure: Rescuing an Overscheduled, Overtested, Underestimated Generation.* New York, NY: Simon & Schuster Paperbacks, 2016.

Benders, David S. "Student Apathy: The Downfall of Education."
ResearchGate. (December 2011).
http://dx.doi.org/10.2139/ssrn.1968613.

Centers for Disease Control and Prevention. "Data and Statistics
on Children's Mental Health | CDC." Last updated March 22,
2021.
https://www.cdc.gov/childrensmentalhealth/data.
html#:~:text=%E2%80%9CEver%20having%20been%20
diagnosed%20with.

Damon, William. *The Path to Purpose: Helping Our Children Find
Their Calling in Life.* New York: Free Press, 2008.

Insel, Thomas. "NIMH Are Children Overmedicated?" *NIMH
(blog).* June 6, 2016.
https://www.nimh.nih.gov/about/directors/thomas-insel/
blog/2014/are-children-overmedicated.

Krasner, Aaron. "CDC: Mental Illness in Children Costs $247
Billion Annually." *Aaron Krasner MD (blog).* May 17, 2013.
https://aaronkrasner.com/2013/05/17/cdc-mental-illness-in-
children-costs-247-billion-annually/.

Lee, Katherine. "What Happens When Parents Pressure Kids to
Get Good Grades." *Verywell Family (blog).* December 27, 2016.
https://www.verywellfamily.com/cons-of-pressuring-kids-to-
get-good-grades-4117600.

"Mental Health Toll of Academic Pressure." Newport Institute.
April 14, 2021.
https://www.newportinstitute.com/resources/mental-
health/academic-pressure/#:~:text=The%20Impact%20
of%20Academic%20Pressure%20on%20Mental%20
Health&text=A%202019%20review%20study%20found.

Miller, Tony. "Partnering for Education Reform." US Department
of Education. Accessed October 15, 2020.
https://www.ed.gov/news/speeches/partnering-education-
reform.

Mishkin, S. "The Social Dilemma + Depression." *The Mental
Health Collective (blog)*. October 7, 2020.
https://themhcollective.com/blog/the-social-dilemma-and-
depression.

Morand, Connor. "Student Apathy: An Inherent Problem in
Schools." Psychology of Education. May 26, 2020.
https://psych3850n.wordpress.com/2020/05/25/student-apathy-
an-inherent-problem-in-schools/.

Nadworny, Elissa. "NPR Choice Page." *NprEd (blog)*.
November 4, 2016.
https://www.npr.org/sections/ed/2016/11/04/500659746/
middle-school-suicides-reach-an-all-time-high.

National Alliance on Mental Illness. "Mental Health by the
Numbers | NAMI: National Alliance on Mental Illness."
March 2021.
https://nami.org/mhstats.

Schutz, Aaron. "Collective Action for Social Change: An Introduction to Community Organizing." *Academia (blog).* February 26, 2011. https://www.academia.edu/250655/Collective_Action_for_Social_Change_An_Introduction_to_Community_Organizing.

Simpson, Christina. "Effects of Standardized Testing on Students' Well-Being." May 2016. https://projects.iq.harvard.edu/files/eap/files/c._simpson_effects_of_testing_on_well_being_5_16.pdf.

Tauscher, Stacia. "It Is Easier to Build Strong Children than to Repair Broken Adults." *Momspresso* (blog). July 20, 2020. https://www.momspresso.com/parenting/4751d241ff8a4f669af1f46f31b94f26/article/it-is-easier-to-build-strong-children-than-to-repair-broken-adults-mg7ft3l5ew1b.

Terada, Youki. "The Science behind Student Stress." *Edutopia* (blog). August 24, 2018. https://www.edutopia.org/article/science-behind-student-stress#:~:text=A%20new%20study%20finds%20that,for%20some%20it%20stays%20high.

US Department of Education. "Schools and Staffing Survey (SASS)." National Center for Education Statistics. 2008. https://nces.ed.gov/surveys/sass/tables/sass0708_035_s1s.asp.

CHAPTER 4

Collins, Lois M. "Nurturing Child's Innate Spiritual Nature Is a Huge Hedge against Depression, Other Woes." *Deseret News (blog)*. April 4, 2016. Nurturing child's innate spiritual nature is a huge hedge against depression, other woes.

"Community Impact." Mindful Schools. September 8, 2020. https://www.mindfulschools.org/ms-community-impact/.

Fisher, Naomi. "The 'How' and 'Why' of the Classroom." *The Psychologist (blog)*. March 10, 2021. https://thepsychologist.bps.org.uk/how-and-why-classroom.

Freire, Paulo. *Pedagogy of the Oppressed*. New York: Bloomsbury Academic, 1970.

Gordon, James S. "Dr. James S Gordon, Founder | the Center for Mind Body Medicine." The Center for Mind-Body Medicine. Accessed June 9, 2021. https://cmbm.org/about/founder/.

Miller, Lisa, and Teresa Barker. *The Spiritual Child: The New Science on Parenting for Health and Lifelong Thriving*. New York: Picador/St. Martin's Press, 2016.

O'Leary, Winnie. "Play-Based Learning: What It Is and Why It Should Be a Part of Every Classroom." *Edmentum (blog)*. October 4, 2019. https://blog.edmentum.com/play-based-learning-what-it-and-why-it-should-be-part-every-classroom.

"The Mind-Body Connection." Johns Hopkins HealthCare
Solutions. The Johns Hopkins University. Accessed June 9,
2021.
https://www.johnshopkinssolutions.com/the-mind-body-
connection/#:~:text=Johns%20Hopkins%20Medicine%20
has%20developed.

Tolle, Eckhart. n.d. "A Quote by Eckhart Tolle." Goodreads.
Accessed June 8, 2021.
https://www.goodreads.com/quotes/69999-being-
spiritual-has-nothing-to-do-with-what-you%20
believe#:~:text="Being%20spiritual%20has%20nothing%20
to%20do%20with%20what%20you%20believe.

CHAPTER 5

Ackoff, Russell. "A Lifetime of Systems Thinking—the Systems
Thinker." The *Systems Thinker (blog)*. November 19, 2015.
https://thesystemsthinker.com/a-lifetime-of-systems-
thinking/.

Baldoni, Justin. "Transcript of 'Why I'm Done Trying to Be 'Man
Enough.'" Filmed 2017. TED video, 18:20.
https://www.ted.com/talks/justin_baldoni_why_i_m_done_
trying_to_be_man_enough/transcript?language=en.

Bigler, Jeff. "The Dvorak Keyboard." www.mit.edu. Last modified
March 7, 2003.
http://www.mit.edu/~jcb/Dvorak/.

Bonchek, Marc. "Why the Problem with Learning Is Unlearning."
Harvard Business Review (Managing Yourself). November 2016.
https://hbr.org/2016/11/why-the-problem-with-learning-is-unlearning.

Jong, Katie De. "The Art of Unlearning: 5 Powerful Myths You
Need to Unlearn to Build a Life You Love." *Medium (blog)*.
April 15, 2019.
https://medium.com/@katiedejong3rd/the-art-of-unlearning-5-powerful-myths-you-need-to-unlearn-to-build-a-life-you-love-8bb367448576.

Harper, Amelia. "Unlearning Is Often a Part of Effective
Teaching." *K-12 Dive (blog)*. May 20, 2019.
https://www.k12dive.com/news/unlearning-is-often-a-part-of-effective-teaching/555066/.

Harris, Victoria. "Neuroplasticity: How I Survived Psychosis and
Jail | NAMI: National Alliance on Mental Illness." *NAMI
(blog)*. March 8, 2021.
https://www.nami.org/Blogs/NAMI-Blog/March-2021/
Neuroplasticity-How-I-Survived-Psychosis-and-Jail?gclid=Cjo
KCQjwna2FBhDPARIsACAEc_UJwprLMR9xh-XIAtGOGsNi
eyanGz8PTc__G_4pdge27vqoj1tYdzIaAuKQEALw_wcB.

Kanwar, Saksham. "The Process of Learning and Unlearning
Through Neuroplasticity." *Medium (blog)*. May 23, 2020.
https://medium.com/swlh/the-process-of-learning-and-unlearning-through-neuroplasticity-d2acb7ecocf2.

Novak, Katie. "What Is UDL? Infographic—Novak Educational Consulting." Www.novakeducation.com. April 19, 2021. https://www.novakeducation.com/blog/what-is-udl-infographic.

Pettinger, Tejvan. "Sunk Cost Fallacy | Economics Help." May 22, 2017. https://www.economicshelp.org/blog/27047/economics/sunk-cost-fallacy/.

Pistorius, Johannes. "After 150 Years, We Should Finally Redesign the Computer Keyboard." *Medium (blog)*. November 24, 2020. https://blog.prototypr.io/after-150-years-we-should-finally-redesign-the-computer-keyboard-d4aa774d7c4b.

CHAPTER 6

Brafman, Rom. "Does Authenticity Lead to Happiness? | Psychology Today." *Psychology Today (blog)*. August 18, 2008. https://www.psychologytoday.com/us/blog/dont-be-swayed/200808/does-authenticity-lead-happiness.

Brown, Brené. *The Gifts of Imperfection: Let Go of Who You Think You're Supposed to Be and Embrace Who You Are*. Charleston, Sc: Instaread Summaries, 2014.

Forleo, Marie. "Dr. Shefali Tsabary: How to Raise Conscious Children." January 2018. In The Marie Forleo Podcast. Podcast. Spotify, 25:00 https://open.spotify.com/pisode/38fDGiasWlZQGv2rVk4WoD.

Harris, Nicole. "How to Raise an Authentic Kid." *Parents (blog)*.
April 10, 2020.
https://www.parents.com/health/healthy-happy-kids/how-to-raise-an-authentic-kid/.

Levitt, Nadine. "Netflix's the Social Dilemma and Lessons for Parents." *Thrive Global (blog)*. November 12, 2020.
https://thriveglobal.com/stories/netflixs-the-social-dilemma-and-lessons-for-parents/.

Schenck, Laura. "Authentic Self vs. False Self—Mindfulness Muse." *Mindfulness Muse (blog)*. April 14, 2011.
https://www.mindfulnessmuse.com/individual-differences/authentic-self-vs-false-self.

Tencer, Daniel. "85% Of Jobs That Will Exist In 2030 Haven't Been Invented Yet: Dell." HuffPost Canada (blog). July 14, 2017.
https://www.huffingtonpost.ca/2017/07/14/85-of-jobs-that-will-exist-in-2030-haven-t-been-invented-yet-d_a_23030098/.

The School of Life. "The True and the False Self." April 19, 2018.
Video, 6:54.
https://www.youtube.com/watch?v=Ao2Ucd6monY.

CHAPTER 7

Brackett, Marc A. *Permission to Feel: Unlocking the Power of Emotions to Help Our Kids, Ourselves, and Our Society Thrive*.
New York: Celadon Books, 2019.

Brieske, Tim. "Emotional Spring Cleaning." *Chopra (blog)*. March 8, 2013.
https://chopra.com/articles/emotional-spring-cleaning.

Elias, Maurice J. "SEL and Spirituality: Instructional Implications." *Edutopia (blog)*. November 14, 2019.
https://www.edutopia.org/blog/social-emotional-learning-and-spirituality-instructional-implications-maurice-elias.

"From a Nation at Risk to a Nation at Hope." A Nation at Hope. October 12, 2018.
http://nationathope.org/report-from-the-nation/.

Goleman, Daniel. *Emotional Intelligence, Why It Can Matter More than IQ & Working with Emotional Intelligence: Omnibus.* London: Bloomsbury, 2004.

Lechner, Tamara. "Emotional Framework: How to Experience Emotions in a Healthy Way." *Chopra (blog)*. December 14, 2018.
https://chopra.com/articles/emotional-framework-how-to-experience-emotions-in-a-healthy-way.

Lin, Judy. "Mrs. Rogers Tells All—Nicely." CBS News. October 8, 2003.
https://www.cbsnews.com/news/mrs-rogers-tells-all-nicely/.

"SEL Impact." CASEL. 2019.
https://casel.org/impact/.

Sowder, Nicolette. *Wilder Child.* Accessed June 25, 2021.
https://wilderchild.com/.

TED. "The Gift and Power of Emotional Courage | Susan David."
February 20, 2018. Video, 16:48.
https://www.youtube.com/watch?v=NDQ1Mi5I4rg.

"World Happiness Report 2019." World Happiness Report.
Accessed March 1, 2021.
https://worldhappiness.report/ed/2019/.

CHAPTER 8

"About ACEs." Compassionate Resilient Schools. 2021.
http://www.compassionateresilientschools.com/about-aces.html.

Branden, Nathaniel. *The Six Pillars of Self-Esteem.* New York;
London: Bantam, 1994.

Minahan, Jessica. "Trauma-Informed Teaching Strategies—
Educational Leadership." *Making School a Safe Place* 77:2
(October 2019): 30-35.
http://www.ascd.org/publications/educational_leadership/oct19/
vol77/num02/Trauma-Informed_Teaching_Strategies.aspx.

Myss, Caroline. "Preparing for Your Inner Journey." *Chopra (blog).*
December 6, 2013.
https://chopra.com/articles/preparing-for-your-inner-journey.

Centers for Disease Control and Prevention. "About the CDC-Kaiser ACE Study | Violence Prevention | Injury Center | CDC." September 3, 2020. https://www.cdc.gov/violenceprevention/aces/about.html?CDC_AA_refVal=https%3A%2F%2Fwww.cdc.gov%2Fviolenceprevention%2Facestudy%2Fabout.html.

Centers for Disease Control and Prevention. "Preventing Adverse Childhood Experiences (ACEs) to Improve U.S. Health." Last reviewed November 5, 2019. https://www.cdc.gov/media/releases/2019/p1105-prevent-aces.html.

Centers for Disease Control and Prevention. "Preventing Adverse Childhood Experiences | Violence Prevention | Injury Center | CDC." September 3, 2020. https://www.cdc.gov/violenceprevention/aces/fastfact.html.

Centers for Disease Control and Prevention. "School Connectedness." Last reviewed August 7, 2018. https://www.cdc.gov/healthyyouth/protective/school_connectedness.htm.

Crosson-Tower, Cynthia. "The Role of Educators in Preventing and Responding to Child Abuse and Neglect." US Department of Health and Human Services. 2004. https://www.childwelfare.gov/pubPDFs/educator.pdf.

Perry, Bruce and Oprah Winfrey. *What Happened to You: Conversations on Trauma, Resilience and Healing.* S.L.: Bluebird, 2021.

TED. "How Childhood Trauma Affects Health across a Lifetime |
    Nadine Burke Harris." February 17, 2015. Video, 16:03.
    https://www.youtube.com/watch?time_
    continue=956&v=95ovIJ3dsNk&feature=emb_logo.

TEDx Talks. "Trauma Not Transformed Is Trauma Transferred |
    Tabitha Mpamira-Kaguri | TEDx Oakland." December 3, 2019.
    Video, 9:09.
    https://www.youtube.com/watch?v=b4loBphYCXI.

Winfrey, Oprah. "Oprah Winfrey Reports on Childhood Trauma
    and How to Treat It." KVC Health Systems (blog). March 12,
    2018.
    https://www.kvc.org/blog/oprah-winfrey-reports-on-
    childhood-trauma/.

Wittels Wachs, Stephanie. "The Last Day—Trauma (with Dr.
    Gabor Mate)." Interview by Stephanie Wittels Wachs. The Last
    Day, Lemonada Media, January 29, 2020. Audio, 47:34.
    https://open.spotify.com/episode/o2g7MOfpU6YZJ17cbmdnBl.

CHAPTER 9

Deats, Sarah. "Love Yourself." Hope Inc. Stories (blog). December
    19, 2019.
    https://hopeinc.com/love-yourself/.

Edutopia. "The Power of Relationships in Schools." January 14,
    2019. Video, 3:40.
    https://www.youtube.com/watch?v=kzvm1m8zq5g.

Skovholt, Thomas M., and Michelle Trotter-Mathison. *The Resilient Practitioner: Burnout Prevention and Self-Care Strategies for Counselors, Therapists, Teachers, and Health Professionals.* New York: Routledge, 2011.

TED. "Every Kid Needs a Champion | Rita Pierson." May 3, 2013. Video, 7:48. https://www.youtube.com/watch?v=SFnMTHhKdkw.

"The Current State of Teacher Burnout in America." School of Education—American University. March 10, 2019. https://soeonline.american.edu/blog/the-current-state-of-teacher-burnout-in-america.

Turner, Cory. "Teachers Are Stressed, And That Should Stress Us All." NPR.org. December 30, 2016. https://www.npr.org/sections/ed/2016/12/30/505432203/teachers-are-stressed-and-that-should-stress-us-all#:~:text=Forty%2Dsix%20percent%20of%20teachers.

"Why Teacher Self-Care Matters and How to Practice Self-Care in Your School | Waterford.org." Waterford.org. June 10, 2019. https://www.waterford.org/education/teacher-self-care-activities/.

CHAPTER 10

Harper, Craig. "Are You Living Consciously in an Unconscious World?" *Lifehack (blog).* Accessed May 3, 2021. https://www.lifehack.org/articles/lifehack/are-you-living-consciously-in-an-unconscious-world.html.

Jorgensen, Larry M. "Seventeenth-Century Theories of Consciousness." Edited by Edward N. Zalta. Stanford Encyclopedia of Philosophy. Metaphysics Research Lab, Stanford University. 2020. https://plato.stanford.edu/entries/consciousness-17th/#DescCons.

"Research on Mindfulness in Ed." Mindful Schools. 2019. https://www.mindfulschools.org/about-mindfulness/research-on-mindfulness/.

"Use of Yoga and Meditation Becoming More Popular in US." CDC/ National Center for Health Statistics. 2019. https://www.cdc.gov/nchs/pressroom/nchs_press_releases/2018/201811_Yoga_Meditation.htm.

World Government Summit. "How Consciousness Can Transform Education— Full Session—WGS 2019." February 10, 2019. Video, 29:13. https://www.youtube.com/watch?v=-mr4D8Jfj1E.

CHAPTER 11

Brame, C.J., and B. Dewsbury. "LSE Resources." LSE Resources. 2017. https://lse.ascb.org/evidence-based-teaching-guides/inclusive-teaching/developing-self-awareness/.

Chopra, Deepak. *What Are You Hungry For? The Chopra Solution to Permanent Weight Loss, Well-Being, and Lightness of Soul.* London: Rider Books, 2015.

"SEL for Adults: Self-Awareness and Self-Management." Greater Good in Education. 2021. https://ggie.berkeley.edu/my-well-being/sel-for-adults-self-awareness-and-self-management/.

Tony, Team. "How to Be Honest with Yourself | Tony Robbins." Tonyrobbins.com. February 18, 2021. https://www.tonyrobbins.com/mind-meaning/be-honest-with-yourself/.

UCSF. "Unconscious Bias | Diversity.ucsf.edu." UCSF.edu. 2016. https://diversity.ucsf.edu/resources/unconscious-bias.

CHAPTER 12

Campbell, Colin. "Jay Shetty: Life of Thought." *Medium (blog)*. March 25, 2018. https://medium.com/lifeofthought/jay-shetty-life-of-thought-f7925a5ac11b.

Derler, Andrea, and Jennifer Ray. "Why Change Is So Hard—and How to Deal with It." NeuroLeadership Institute. December 12, 2019. https://neuroleadership.com/your-brain-at-work/growth-mindset-deal-with-change.

Dweck, Carol S. *Mindset*. London: Robinson, 2017.

Reis, Rick "Mindsets and Resistance to Learning | Tomorrow's Professor Postings." Tomprof.stanford.edu. 2017. https://tomprof.stanford.edu/posting/1649.

CONCLUSION

Detoro, Robyn. "5 Statements from Mandela That We Should All Be Inspired By." *ONE (blog).* July 18, 2018. https://www.one.org/us/blog/nelson-mandala-quotes-inspiration/.